Crime and Punishment

Fyodor Dostoyevsky

Abridged and adapted by Joanne Suter

Illustrated by James McConnell

A PACEMAKER CLASSIC

Fearon Education
Belmont, California

Simon & Schuster Supplementary Education Group

Other Pacemaker Classics

The Adventures of Huckleberry Finn
The Adventures of Tom Sawyer
The Deerslayer
Dr. Jekyll and Mr. Hyde
Frankenstein
Great Expectations
Jane Eyre
The Jungle Book
The Last of the Mohicans
Moby Dick
The Moonstone
Robinson Crusoe
The Scarlet Letter
A Tale of Two Cities
The Three Musketeers
The Time Machine
Treasure Island
20,000 Leagues Under the Sea
Two Years Before the Mast

Library of Congress Catalog Card Number: 90-82222

ISBN 0–8224–9353–5

Printed in the United States of America

1. 9 8 7 6 5 4 3 2 1

Contents

1 The Plot

It was a very hot evening early in July. A young man came out onto the streets of St. Petersburg. It seemed as if he did not want to get to the place he was going.

The young man had been careful to avoid his landlady when he left his shabby room. He did not want to hear her silly chatter. He had things on his mind. He was so very poor. He had to get some money. He had to think about his plan.

The heat on the street was terrible. The lack of air, the dust, and the smell of the city all pressed down upon him. He had hardly eaten for two days, and he felt weak. He lived in a bad part of the city, but even there his dress seemed very shabby. The young man was, by the way, extremely handsome. He was tall, slim, and well-built. He had beautiful dark eyes and dark brown hair. Now he sank deep into thought as he walked slowly along the streets.

He stopped when he came to a huge house which stood beside a canal. The house had been divided into many tiny apartments. The man slipped into one of the doors. His heart pounded as he went up a dark, narrow back staircase to the fourth floor.

"If I am so scared now, how would I feel if I were really going to do *it?*" he asked himself.

Suddenly his way was blocked by some movers who were carrying furniture. They were moving people out of a large flat.

"It is a good thing," the young man said to himself. "Now the floor will be empty except for the old woman's flat." He moved slowly to the door of the woman's flat. He rang the bell. His nerves were on edge, and even the bell's sound startled him.

In a little while, the door was opened a tiny crack. The old woman eyed her visitor through the open space. Nothing could be seen but her narrow eyes glittering in the darkness.

The old woman knew her visitor, so she opened the door wider. The young man stepped into the dark entry. The old woman was tiny, about 60 years old. She had a sharp little nose and colorless hair. She wore an old fur cape even though it was very hot. She coughed and groaned, and peered at the young man.

"Remember me?" he said carefully. "I am Raskolnikov, a student. I came here a month ago. I have something more to pawn."

"I remember you," the old woman said. She did not take her eyes from Raskolnikov's face. She waited a bit. "Step in," she said at last.

Raskolnikov entered the room. He looked about carefully, trying to remember everything about it. She was a messy old woman, but the apartment was surprisingly clean. "Lizaveta's work," Raskolnikov thought. Lizaveta was the woman's younger sister. She lived with the old woman and took care of her. Lizaveta seemed to be out that day.

"What do you want?" the old woman asked.

Raskolnikov took a silver watch out of his pocket. "How much will you give me for the watch, Alyona Ivanovna?" he asked.

"A ruble and a half," she said.

"A ruble and a half!" the young man cried, shocked by the poor offer.

"Please yourself." Alyona Ivanovna tried to hand him back the watch.

Raskolnikov was so angry he wanted to run away. But he stopped himself. He remembered the real reason he had come. "I'll take it," he said roughly.

The old woman went into her bedroom to get the money. Raskolnikov listened carefully. He could hear her unlocking a chest of drawers. "It must be in there," he thought. "Her money must be locked in the chest. And she carries the keys with her."

Alyona Ivanovna came back and handed Raskolnikov the money. He took it. "I may be bringing you something else in a day or two, Alyona Ivanovna," he said. "A valuable thing, a silver cigarette box. I will see you then." He prepared to leave, and then he looked about. "Are you always home alone? Your sister is not here with you?" he asked as if it were unimportant.

"What business is that of yours, my good sir?" asked the old woman.

"Oh, none, I suppose," Raskolnikov answered. "I simply asked. Good day, Alyona Ivanovna."

Raskolnikov went out. He stopped several times going down the stairs. He felt confused. He had to catch his breath.

When he was out in the street he cried out loud. "How terrible it all is! Can I? Can I possibly?" He walked along the street like a drunken man. He moved quickly, as if trying to escape. He did not stop until he reached the next street.

Then he stopped and looked around. He found himself standing by a tavern. Until that moment, he had never been into a tavern. Suddenly he felt thirsty. He wanted a drink of cold beer.

Raskolnikov went down the stairs into the tavern. He sat down at a sticky little table in a dark corner and ordered a beer. He quickly drank the first glass, and he felt better. He looked around the room. There were very few people in the tavern, but one man caught his attention. The man was sitting alone, sipping from his beer, and looking around at the others in the room. He, too, appeared to be very upset.

Raskolnikov was not usually friendly. He did, in fact, not want the company of others, especially lately. But suddenly he felt a need to be with other people. He wanted something to take his mind off his own, terrible plot.

Raskolnikov stared at the man. He decided the man was some sort of retired government clerk. He was over 50 and bald. He was of medium height and stoutly built. His face had a yellowish color and was puffy from too much drink. But Raskolnikov thought that something in the man's little reddish eyes looked rather smart. His clothing was shabby. What had once been a black dress coat was now a rag without buttons. Like a clerk, he wore no beard. He rested his elbows on the sticky table and looked back at Raskolnikov.

At last he spoke, loudly. "Would you like, sir, some conversation? Marmeladov is my name. You appear to be a man of education. Are you a clerk?"

"No, I am studying," Raskolnikov answered.

"A student then, or formerly a student," cried Marmeladov. He got up and staggered toward Raskolnikov. He sat down at his table and began pouring out the story of his unhappy life.

"I, sir, am a scoundrel," he cried. "My wife, Katerina Ivanovna, is a person of education. She is a lady. But

I am a pig, a beast. Do you know sir, that I have sold her very stockings for drink? We live in a cold room. She caught cold this winter and began coughing and spitting blood. We have three little children. Katerina cares for them from morning until night, washing and scrubbing, but she is very ill. And I continue to drink, spending all we have.

"For a while I tried to stay away from this," Marmeladov continued as he tapped his beer glass. "But I lost my job. We have a small room now, and what we live upon and with what we pay our rent I could not say. I don't know what we would do if not for Sonia."

Raskolnikov showed no real interest, but Marmeladov went on. "Sonia is my daughter by my first wife. Sonia, as you might imagine, has no education. What she knows, she has read and learned on her own.

"One day, the children were hungry, Katerina was very ill, and I was lying drunk on the bed. I saw Sonia get up and go out. When she came back later, she laid 30 rubles on the table before Katerina. She did not say a word. She lay down on the bed with her face to the wall. She covered herself with a big, green shawl. Her little shoulders and body kept shaking. Then Katerina went over to Sonia, knelt down beside her, and put her arms around her. They stayed like that together all night while I lay drunk.

7

Sonia had become a prostitute. She had sold herself so that the children might have food, and we might have rent.

"And now I've left them. I've even stolen what money Katerina had to buy more beer. Sonia can no longer live with Katerina and the children. Her shame is too great. My daughter has given me money. In fact, I am drinking with it right now. Who will have pity on a man like me?"

Marmeladov put his head down on the dirty table. Then suddenly he raised his head and spoke to Raskolnikov. "Come along with me. I'm going to Katerina. It is time I did."

Raskolnikov saw that the man needed help. Marmeladov was very unsteady on his feet. He leaned on Raskolnikov as they made their way into the street. Marmeladov became even more upset as they got closer to his house.

"It is not what Katerina will say that frightens me," he said. "It is not that she will shout and pull my hair. It is her eyes . . . and her breathing. Have you noticed how sick people breathe when they are excited? Blows I am not afraid of. Let her strike me. It is better so."

When they reached Marmeladov's house they went up some dark stairs to the fourth floor. A little door stood open at the top of the stairs. Through the open door, Raskolnikov could see a poor-looking room lighted by a single candle. He recognized Katerina Ivanovna at once. She was a tall woman. She was terribly thin and hungry looking, and she had red cheeks flushed with fever. Three thin children were in the room as well. They stared out of big, dark eyes.

Marmeladov dropped on his knees in the doorway. Katerina took no notice of Raskolnikov. She saw her husband and cried out. "He has come back! The monster! And where is the money? You've drunk it all, and they are hungry!" She pointed to the children.

Suddenly Katerina turned to Raskolnikov. "Are you not ashamed?" she cried. "You have been drinking with him. Go away!"

Raskolnikov hurried to leave. He could hear Katerina shouting at Marmeladov. He saw her pulling him about by his hair. Just as he went out, Raskolnikov had time to put his hand into his pocket. He snatched up the change he had gotten from his ruble in the tavern and laid it on the window ledge. Afterward, on the stairs, he changed his mind and wished he could go back.

"What a stupid thing I've done in giving them money," he thought. "They have Sonia, and I want it myself."

2 Working Out the Plan

Raskolnikov woke up late the next day. He had slept poorly. He looked with hatred at his room. It was the size of a cupboard, shabby, with dusty yellow paper peeling off the walls. It was an attic room with a low ceiling. Raskolnikov always felt he might easily knock his head against it. An old sofa covered with rags served as a bed.

But the room was a place Raskolnikov could hide away from the world. Only the building's servant girl, Nastasya, bothered him there.

"Get up. Why are you asleep?" Nastasya called to him that morning as she came to his room. "It's past nine, and I have brought you some tea."

She set before him a cracked teapot full of weak and stale tea. Then she sat down and began talking.

"The landlady means to complain to the police about you," she said. "You don't pay your rent, and you won't leave the room."

"The landlady is a fool," Raskolnikov replied.

"But why do you lie here like a sack?" Nastasya asked. "You used to go out. You used to teach children. Now, you do nothing."

"I am doing . . . work," he said.

"What sort of work?" Nastasya asked. "What do you want? A fortune all at once?"

"Yes," Raskolnikov answered. Then he gave her a strange look. "Yes," he said again, "I want a fortune."

"Don't be in such a hurry," Nastasya said. "You know, you quite frighten me. But I have forgotten," she continued. "A letter came for you yesterday."

"A letter, for me?" cried Raskolnikov, greatly excited. "Give it to me, for God's sake."

Raskolnikov turned pale when he took the letter. It was from his mother.

"Nastasya, leave me alone. Hurry! Go!"

The letter shook in Raskolnikov's hand. When Nastasya had gone, he lifted it to his lips and kissed it. When he opened the letter, two sheets of paper fell out.

"My dear son," wrote his mother. "It has been two months since I last heard from you. I worry since you have given up your studies at the university and are no longer teaching lessons. I am sorry I cannot send you any money. I had to borrow the last 15 rubles I sent.

"Your sister Dounia is living with me again. She had a very hard time working in the Svidrigailovs' house. That crazy Mr. Svidrigailov was attracted to Dounia right from the very start. At last, he lost all control and made shameful suggestions to Dounia. Svidrigailov's wife overheard. She blamed Dounia.

For a whole month, the town was full of talk about Dounia. Dounia and I dared not even go to church because of the whispers and stares.

"Fortunately, Mr. Svidrigailov has confessed that Dounia did nothing wrong. His wife has since told everyone that she made a terrible mistake in accusing your sister.

"Our fortunes are, indeed, improving. Dounia has agreed to marry someone. Although the matter has been arranged without your advice, I think you will approve. He is a well-to-do man who has already made his fortune. It is true that he is 45 years old, but he is very respectable. His name is Luzhin. Of course, there is no great love on his side or on hers. But Dounia is a clever girl and will make a good wife.

"Luzhin has made it clear that he wants a poor wife, one who will depend entirely upon her husband. This fact bothers Dounia, but she still plans to marry Luzhin.

"Mr. Luzhin will be coming to your city, St. Petersburg, to do some legal work. He hopes to get to know you. In fact, Dounia and I hope Luzhin will find work for you in his office.

"Now that Dounia is engaged to Luzhin, our fortunes are improving. I'll be able to send you some money soon. I send you a mother's blessing."

Yours till death,
Pulcheria Raskolnikov

While he read the letter, Raskolnikov's face was wet with tears. But when he finished it, he was pale. He felt he must get out of his little room. He went onto the streets, talking to himself aloud. Many passersby thought that he was drunk.

"Never such a marriage while I am alive," he muttered. "Never to Luzhin! She is giving up herself for the sake of her family. She is marrying a selfish man she does not love!"

Raskolnikov's bitterness grew stronger. If he had happened to meet Luzhin at that moment, he might have murdered him.

Raskolnikov stopped walking and stood absolutely still. "It shall not be! This marriage will not be!"

Then he looked around. "Where am I going?" he wondered. "I came out for something."

Raskolnikov remembered that he had wanted to see Razumihin, one of his few friends at the university. He had gotten along well with Razumihin. It was nearly impossible to do otherwise, for Razumihin was an especially good-natured, bright fellow. Like Raskolnikov, he was very good looking— tall, thin, and black-haired. Nothing appeared to get Razumihin down. He was poor, but he seemed to be happy living anywhere.

Now Raskolnikov found himself on the way to his old friend's lodgings. "Why?" he asked himself. And he could not answer.

"Do I expect Razumihin to stop me from carrying out my plan?" he wondered. He turned away from Razumihin's street. "No, I shall go to Razumihin's, but not now. I shall go to him on the day after *it*. "

On his way home, Raskolnikov passed through the Hay Market. There he happened to see Lizaveta, the sister of the old pawnbroker. Lizaveta was talking to a man and woman.

"Come around tomorrow, about seven," they were saying to her. "We will have a cup of tea."

"All right. I'll come," Lizaveta answered.

Raskolnikov heard no more. He passed by. He felt a shiver of horror run down his spine. He had quite unexpectedly learned that the next day at seven o'clock, Lizaveta would be away from home. At seven o'clock the old woman *would be left alone.*

He felt suddenly as if the whole thing had been decided for him. The next day the old woman, whose life he planned to take, would be at home completely alone.

When Raskolnikov returned from the Hay Market, he threw himself on his bed and slept deeply. He slept all night and even into the next afternoon.

A striking clock woke him. He jumped up wide awake. He tip-toed to the door and listened. His heart beat terribly fast. All was quiet on the stairs.

It was time to act out his plan. His heart kept thumping so that he could hardly breathe. First, he had to make a noose and sew it into his overcoat. He tore a strip from an old shirt. He folded the strip in two and sewed it inside his coat, under the left armhole. His hands shook as he sewed. But the noose was necessary. He could not pass through the streets carrying an axe in his hands. Now the axe would hang out of sight under his arm on the inside of his coat.

From a little opening between the sofa and the floor Raskolnikov took out a piece of wood. It was about the size of a cigarette case. He wrapped it in white paper and tied it with thread. He tied it again so that it would be hard to untie.

Then he went to his door and started down the steps, quietly, like a cat. He still had the most important thing to do. He had to steal the axe from the kitchen. The deed must be done with an axe. He had decided that long ago.

But the kitchen was locked! Rage boiled inside Raskolnikov. "I have lost my chance forever," he muttered.

Then from an open storeroom across the hall, something shiny caught his eye. There it was, just under the bench. An axe! Raskolnikov dashed to the axe and pulled it from under the bench. He thrust it beneath his coat.

"When reason fails, the devil helps!" he thought.

Once outside, Raskolnikov walked along the streets silently. He did not want anyone to notice him. He saw a clock in a shop window. It was ten past seven! He had to hurry. He walked faster. Suddenly a clock somewhere struck once. "What! Was it half past seven? Impossible, it must be fast."

Raskolnikov arrived at the old woman's building. He pressed his hand against his throbbing heart. He felt the axe under his coat. He began to climb the stairs. The stairs were quiet, and he met no one. One flat on the second floor was open. Painters were at work inside, but they did not glance at him.

Then he reached the fourth floor. Here was the door. For one instant the thought floated through his mind, "Should I go back?" But he made no answer. He listened at the old woman's door for a long time. He heard nothing. Then he pulled himself together and rang the bell. No answer. The old woman was alone, and perhaps she was afraid to answer. He put his ear to the door. He heard something on the other side—a touch of the lock, a rustle of skirt. He rang again. An instant later he heard the latch being unfastened.

3 Murder

The door opened a tiny crack. Two sharp eyes peered at him.

"Good evening, Alyona Ivanovna," Raskolnikov began. His voice broke and shook. "I have come . . . I have brought something . . . but we better come in . . . to the light."

Without waiting, Raskolnikov passed into the room. The old woman ran after him.

"Good heavens, what do you want? What is it?"

"Why, Alyona Ivanovna, I have brought you something of value. I spoke of it the other day."

The old woman looked at the package, then into the eyes of her visitor. She looked at him so hard that Raskolnikov feared she knew his plans. If she had looked at him like that for another moment, he thought he would have run away. But then she asked, "What is it?"

"It is the silver cigarette case. I spoke of it last time I was here."

She held out her hand and took the package. She fumbled with the strings. "But it is tied up so tightly," she cried. She turned to the window, to the light.

Raskolnikov trembled. His hands felt weak, so weak that he feared he might drop the axe.

"But why is it tied up like this?" the old woman cried and moved toward him.

He had not a minute more to lose. He pulled the axe out and swung it with both arms. Almost without thought, he brought the blunt side of the axe down upon her head.

The old woman was so short that the blow fell on the very top of her skull. She cried out softly and sank in a heap on the floor. She raised one hand to her head. In the other hand she still held the package. Then Raskolnikov hit her again, another blow on the same spot. The blood gushed, and the body fell back. He stepped back and let it fall. He bent over her face. She was dead. Her eyes seemed to be staring into space.

Raskolnikov laid the axe on the ground near the woman's body. He felt in her pocket, trying to avoid the streaming blood. He felt clear-headed. He knew what he was doing. But he was shaking. He pulled the keys from her pocket and ran into the bedroom with them.

He fit the keys into a lock on the chest of drawers. When he heard the jingling of the keys he was suddenly shaken. He thought of giving it all up and going away. But the thought passed. It was too late to go back.

Then another terrifying thought came to him. The old woman might still be alive! Leaving the keys in the chest, he ran back to the body. He picked up the axe and held it over the old woman. But he did not bring it down. There was no question. She was dead. Her head was broken and battered, and there was a perfect pool of blood.

All at once Raskolnikov noticed a string on her neck. He cut the string with the axe and pulled it from her body, smearing his hand and the axe with blood. On the string were two crosses, one of wood and one of copper. There was also a tiny silver figure and a small, greasy leather purse. The purse was stuffed very full. Raskolnikov stuck the purse in his pocket and tossed the crosses on the old woman's body. Then he rushed back into the bedroom, taking the axe with him.

He tried to unlock the chest of drawers, but the keys would not work. He left the chest and began searching the room. He found a good-sized box under the bed. The biggest key fit its lock, and he opened it. In the box Raskolnikov found various items made out of gold—bracelets, chains, earrings, pins, and such. He began filling his pockets with the items.

Suddenly he heard steps in the room where the old woman lay. He stopped short and was as still as death. All was quiet. He must have imagined it. Then he heard a faint cry, a low moan. He sat on the floor by the box and waited holding his breath. Suddenly he jumped up, grabbed the axe, and ran out of the bedroom.

In the middle of the room stood Lizaveta. She was staring at her murdered sister. She was as white as a sheet. She did not seem to have the strength to cry out. Seeing Raskolnikov run out of the bedroom, she began shaking all over. She opened her mouth, but still she did not scream. She began slowly backing away from him into the corner. He rushed at her with the axe. Lizaveta held up one hand as if to motion him away. Raskolnikov brought the axe down with the sharp edge on her skull. She fell heavily.

Raskolnikov was filled with fear after this second, unexpected murder. He wanted to run away. Then a sort of blankness, a dreaminess, came over him. He forgot the horrors of his crime and became concerned with the smallest things. Seeing a bucket of water in the kitchen, he went to wash away the blood. He carefully washed his hands and cleaned the axe. Then he hung the axe once more beneath his coat.

"I must get away, get away," he thought. He opened the door and listened on the stairs. He was just taking a step toward the stairs when he heard footsteps. They were coming . . . the first floor . . . the third floor . . .

Raskolnikov slipped quickly back into the flat and closed the door behind him. He quietly fixed the latch. Then he waited behind the door, holding his breath, listening.

The visitor rang the bell loudly. Then he rang again, and then he shook the door handle.

"What's up? Are they asleep?" shouted an angry voice. "Hey, Alyona Ivanovna. Lizaveta. Open the door!"

Raskolnikov heard other footsteps. Someone else was approaching. "Do you think there is no one home?" the second visitor called.

"There must be someone there," the first man said. "I can feel that the door is not locked from the outside, but merely latched on the inside. At least one of them must be at home."

"There must be something wrong," the second man said. "Either they have both fainted or . . ."

"What?"

"Let us go find the landlord. Let him wake them up."

Raskolnikov kept tight hold of the axe. He felt as if he were in a dream. While the two men were talking and knocking, he had, several times, felt like shouting back at them. When he heard them go away, he unfastened the latch and opened the door. There was no sound. Quickly, without any thought at all, he went out. He closed the door behind him and went down the stairs.

He had gone down two flights when he suddenly heard footsteps coming up the stairs. They were coming back. They were only a flight below him. If they saw him, they might stop him. If not, they would surely remember him. All was lost.

Then suddenly, a few steps away, he saw an empty flat with the door wide open. It was the flat on the second floor where painters had been at work. It was as though they had left the door open just for him. He dashed into the room and hid behind a wall. He waited until the footsteps on the stairs had gone on by. He heard them going up, up to the fourth floor. Then he went out on tiptoe and ran down the stairs. No one was on the stairs now. He walked into the street and turned left.

He knew that by now they had returned to the flat. By now they were looking at the bodies. He went on. He was weak now, and sweat ran down him in drops.

Raskolnikov was in a daze by the time he arrived home. He had already started up to his room when he remembered the axe. He had to return it. He carefully put it back under the bench where he had found it. He met no one, not a soul, on the way to his room. When he was inside, he flung himself on the sofa fully dressed. He did not sleep. Thoughts crowded his brain. Then his mind sank into a dark blankness.

4 A Summons from the Police

Raskolnikov lay that way for a very long while. At last he heard noise from the street below his window. Then, in a flash, he remembered everything. A chill came over him. He began shaking. His teeth chattered. He thought he must be going mad. But the chill was from the fever that had begun in his sleep.

Raskolnikov looked around with surprise. He wondered how he could have come in without locking the door. How had he flung himself on the sofa without undressing?

He began looking himself over from head to foot. Were there no traces? A few drops of dried blood were on the ragged edge of his pants. He picked up a knife and cut off the threads.

Suddenly he remembered the purse and the other things he had taken from the old woman's flat. They were still in his pockets! He rushed to take them out. He carried the heap to a corner of his room. There, a piece of wallpaper had peeled away from a hole in the wall. He began stuffing all the things in the hole under the paper. "They're in! All out of sight!"

He sat down down on the sofa, completely worn out. He covered himself with his ragged coat and, once more, fell into a deep sleep.

Not more than five minutes had passed when he jumped up. "How could I have gone to sleep? I have not taken the loop off the armhole! I forgot the loop that carried the axe! Such a clue!"

He pulled off the loop, and then he quickly cut it to pieces and hid the bits under his pillow. He looked around. Had he forgotten anything? He felt his powers of thinking were failing him.

"Surely it isn't beginning already! Surely it isn't my punishment coming upon me. It is!"

Then he looked down at his boots. He pulled one off. The sock was soaked with blood. He must have stepped in the pool by the woman's body.

"What am I to do with the bloody sock? I had better throw it away somewhere. Yes, throw it away," he repeated. He sat down, and his head sank on the pillow. Shaking came over him. "Perhaps I should go off somewhere right now and throw it all away," he thought.

Several times he tried to rise from the sofa. But he could not. Then he was startled by a hard knocking at his door.

"Open up, will you? Are you dead or alive?" The serving girl, Nastasya, was shouting and banging on the door.

Raskolnikov half rose. He leaned forward. His room was so small he could undo the latch without leaving the bed.

Nastasya entered. She stared at him in a strange way. She held out a gray folded paper sealed with wax. "A notice from the police office," she said.

"From the police? What for?"

Nastasya looked at Raskolnikov closely. "You are downright ill!" she said. "You have a fever!"

Raskolnikov did not answer. He held the paper without opening it. Nastasya seemed to feel sorry for him. "You're ill. You cannot go. Why, what do you have there?"

Raskolnikov looked. He was holding the bloody sock. Quickly he pushed it under his coat.

"I'll bring you some tea," Nastasya said.

"No, I'm going at once." Raskolnikov got to his feet.

"As you please," Nastasya said. She went out.

Raskolnikov rushed to the light to examine the sock.

"There are stains," he thought. "But they are covered with dirt. Nastasya could not have noticed."

Then, shaking, he broke the seal on the paper and began reading. It was a notice to appear at the police station.

"Why today?" Raskolnikov wondered. "Why? I have never had anything to do with the police!"

He began dressing. "The sock! Shall I put it on?"

He put it on, then pulled it off again in horror. But he had no other socks. He put it on again—and laughed. But his laughter was followed by fear. His legs shook and he felt light-headed. "I might blurt out something," he thought worriedly.

Raskolnikov went out. In the street the heat was terrible again. He felt his head going round.

"If they question me, perhaps I'll simply tell," he thought as he drew near the police station. "I'll go in, fall on my knees, and confess everything," he thought as he climbed the stairs to the office.

Inside the office, the heat was worse than on the street. There was a sickening smell of fresh paint from newly decorated rooms.

A clerk looked at him. "What do you want?"

"I was called here . . . by a notice," Raskolnikov mumbled.

The clerk looked through some papers. "For money due," the clerk said. He tossed a paper to Raskolnikov. "Read that!"

"Money? What money?" thought Raskolnikov. "But then, it is certainly not *that.*" And he trembled with joy. A load was lifted from his mind.

Raskolnikov read the paper, but he did not understand.

"What is this?" he asked.

"It is a notice of rent money owed by you to your landlady. You must make payment or sign an IOU promising to make payment before you leave the station."

Just then Raskolnikov noticed the chief of police talking to an investigator named Porfiry. Their words reached him.

"The murderer must have been there when they knocked. He must have slipped by them somehow."

Raskolnikov shook so much that he could hardly hold the pen as he signed the paper. When he finished, he did not get up. He put his head in his hands. He felt as if a nail were being driven into his head. A strange idea came to him. He would tell everything that had happened. He would take the police to his room and show them the things in the hole in the corner.

Then Raskolnikov got up and walked toward the door. But he did not reach it.

He fainted. When he came to, he found himself sitting in a chair. Investigator Porfiry was offering him a glass of yellowish water.

"Are you ill?" the investigator asked. "Have you been ill long?"

"Since yesterday," Raskolnikov answered.

"Did you go out yesterday?"

"Yes."

"At what time?"

"At about seven."

"You were ill, and yet you went out? And where did you go, may I ask?"

"Just along the street."

Raskolnikov was now as white as a handkerchief. He stared with feverish eyes. There was a long silence.

"Very well, then," Porfiry said suddenly. "We will not keep you."

Raskolnikov went out. He heard conversation behind him as he left. He felt terror. "They suspect! There will be a search!"

In his room again, he looked about. Nothing had been touched. He rushed to the corner, put his hand under the paper, and pulled the items out. He put everything in his pockets.

"I will fling everything into a canal. The thing will be at an end." He went out without closing the door behind him.

Raskolnikov wandered along the banks of the canal. But there were too many people around to carry out his plan.

In a park he spied a deserted stone shed. He slipped inside the shed. He bent down over a loose stone. Under the stone was a small hollow. He emptied his pockets into it. The old woman's purse lay on top. He twisted the stone back into place. Nothing could be noticed.

Then he went out. For an instant he was filled with joy. "Who would think of looking under that stone? It is all over. No clue!" And he laughed. Then he stopped. A new question came to him. "How is it that I did not even look into the purse? Did I even want the money? It is because I am ill," he decided. "I don't know what I am doing."

He walked on. Soon he found himself in front of his friend Razumihin's house. He was not sure if he had come on purpose or by chance.

"I said I would come and see him on the day *after,*" Raskolnikov thought. "And so I will. Besides, I am too weak to go any farther."

He went up to Razumihin's room. Razumihin was wearing a ragged robe and old slippers. His face showed surprise.

"Is it you after so long a time?" he cried. "Come sit down. You look tired." Razumihin looked at his visitor. "You have a fever."

Suddenly, seeing his friend face to face, Raskolnikov was angry at himself. Why had he come?

"Good-bye," he said. He walked to the door.

"Stop!" Razumihin cried. "Why the devil have you come? Are you mad or something? I won't let you go like that!"

"I came to you because I knew no one but you who could help," Raskolnikov began. "But now I see I am by myself. Leave me alone!"

But Razumihin would not turn away from an old friend. "Take these three rubles," he insisted.

Raskolnikov took the money and, without a word, went out. But on the next street, he turned back. He climbed the stairs to Razumihin's flat again. He laid the rubles on his friend's table and went out without speaking a word.

"Are you mad?" Razumihin shouted after him. "What did you come to see me for?"

Raskolnikov did not answer. He stumbled home and, once again, he fell into a deep sleep.

He was in a fever. Sometimes he was half awake, sometimes in a deep sleep. At last, he woke up completely. Sun shone into the room. He saw that Razumihin was there.

"It is a good thing you are awake," Razumihin cried. "And it is lucky I came here. For the last four days you have had almost nothing to eat or drink. I have given you a little tea by spoonfuls. I brought the doctor, Zossimov, to see you twice. He said it was nothing serious. He said something seemed to have gone to your head. He could not quite give it a name.

A messenger has come here, too." Razumihin continued. "He brought 35 rubles to you from your mother."

"I don't want the money," Raskolnikov muttered.

"Don't want the money? Come, brother, that is nonsense," said Razumihin.

"Were you here all the time I slept?" asked Raskolnikov. "Did I say anything in my sleep?"

"I should think so! You were beside yourself."

"What did I say?"

"You said something about earrings and chains. And you cried, 'Give me my sock!' Zossimov and I hunted all about the room. Only when we gave the sock to you were you quiet.

"Now," Razumihin continued, "to the business at hand. I will take 10 of the 35 rubles and buy some things you need."

When Razumihin had left the room, Raskolnikov flung himself out of bed like a madman. "What if they know? I must escape. Where are my clothes? What's this? A half a bottle of beer left?" He gulped the beer. His thoughts grew more unclear. Sleepiness came over him.

When he woke, Razumihin had returned. He had brought Raskolnikov some new clothes—some gray summer pants and a waistcoat to match.

"What money was all that bought with?" asked Raskolnikov.

"Money? Why, the money your mother sent."

The door opened and a tall, stout man came in. He looked familiar to Raskolnikov.

"Zossimov! At last!" cried Razumihin in delight.

5 Raskolnikov's Illness

Zossimov was 27 years old. He had a puffy, pale, clean-shaven face. He wore glasses and a big, gold ring on his fat finger. The doctor dressed very well. He seemed quite pleased with himself. This high opinion of himself bothered many who knew him. However, most people did think he was a clever doctor.

"And how do we feel now?" Zossimov asked Raskolnikov.

"He still seems quite unhappy," Razumihin said.

"I am well. I am perfectly well!" Raskolnikov declared. He raised himself on the sofa and looked at them with glittering eyes. Then he sank back and turned to the wall.

"I would like to take him out," Razumihin said. "I am having a little party. He could come. He could lie on the sofa. It might do him good. You are coming, I hope," he said to Zossimov

"And who will be there?" the doctor asked.

"Just our friends. A few neighbors. And my uncle. Porfiry is his name. He is 65. I am very fond of him. He is the head of the Investigation Department here.

He is working on a murder case, the murder of an old pawnbroker. A painter, a house painter, is mixed up in it."

"Oh, I read about that murder in the papers. I was rather interested in it," Zossimov said. "Another woman, Lizaveta, was murdered as well."

"Lizaveta," Raskolnikov whispered. He stared at the wall, at the dirty, yellow paper. He felt his arms and legs as lifeless as if they had been cut off. He did not move.

"But what about the painter?" Zossimov asked.

"He is accused of the murder," Razumihin went on.

"Was there evidence against him?"

"No good evidence," said Razumihin. "The painter was found with some earrings in a jewel box. The jewelry and the box belonged to the murdered pawnbroker. The man insists he found the box on the floor behind the door when he was painting the flat."

"Behind the door? Lying behind the door?" Raskolnikov cried suddenly. He stared with a look of terror at Razumihin. He sat up on the sofa.

"Yes . . . why? What's the matter?"

"Nothing," Raskolnikov answered faintly. He turned to the wall again.

"He must have awakened from a dream," said Razumihin.

"Well, go on," said Zossimov. "What next?"

"The painter's story could be true, Razumihin said. The real murderer might have dropped the jewel box!"

At that moment, the door opened, and a stranger came in. He stopped short in the doorway and stared about him. He was a gentleman who was no longer young. He stood stiffly as if he did not trust anyone. With a look of surprise, his eyes rested on Raskolnikov, who lay undressed and unwashed on the dirty sofa. Then he looked at the rumpled, unshaven Razumihin. There was silence.

The stranger then addressed Zossimov. "I am looking for Raskolnikov, a student, or formerly a student?"

Razumihin answered. "He is there, lying on the sofa. What do you want?"

Raskolnikov himself lay without speaking, staring at the stranger. Suddenly he jumped up. "Yes, I am Raskolnikov! What do you want?"

The visitor looked at him, and then he said loudly, "I am Luzhin. I believe you have heard of me."

Raskolnikov sank back without a word.

Luzhin began to explain, "Your mamma sent a letter to you. She said I was coming."

"I know!" cried Raskolnikov. "So, you are the one who plans to marry my sister!"

Raskolnikov stared at Luzhin again. The man had dressed to make a good impression. All his clothes were brand-new, even the lavender gloves he carried in his hand. He dressed to look younger than his 45 years. His hair was carefully combed and curled. After looking Luzhin over, Raskolnikov grinned an ugly grin, sank back, and stared at the ceiling.

"I am sorry to find you ill," Luzhin said, breaking the silence. "I am expecting your mamma and sister in St. Petersburg. I have found a lodging for them."

"Where?" asked Raskolnikov weakly.

"Very near here, in a house rented out by a merchant named Yushin."

"I've been there," Razumihin said. "It is a filthy place. It's cheap, though."

"I could not find out much about it myself," Luzhin replied. "I am a stranger in St. Petersburg. It is for only a short time."

Luzhin turned to Raskolnikov. "I trust we will get to know each other better when you are well."

Raskolnikov did not turn his head to look at Luzhin. Zossimov took up the conversation that Luzhin had interrupted. He spoke of the murder again. "One of her customers might have killed her," he declared.

"Not a doubt about that," replied Razumihin. "Porfiry is examining all who have sold her goods. He has their names from records in her rooms. Some of the customers have come forward themselves."

"It must have been a clever, experienced criminal," Zossimov said. "The boldness of it! The coldness!"

"That's just what it wasn't," said Razumihin. "I believe he was not experienced. Probably that was his first crime. They found money and jewels left in the room. He did not know how to rob. He could only murder. It was his first crime, I assure you. He lost his head. He got away more by luck than by planning."

Raskolnikov lay on the sofa with a white face. His upper lip was twitching. He seemed very excited. He interrupted the conversation, turning to the subject of Luzhin's engagement.

"Is it true," he cried in a voice shaking with fury, "that you told my sister that what pleased you most was that she was a beggar? Did you say it was better to raise a wife from poverty so that you could have complete control over her?"

"Upon my word!" cried Luzhin. "You have changed my words all around. You misunderstand!"

"Go to hell!" cried Raskolnikov. "I shall send you flying down the stairs!"

"So that is how it is?" Luzhin turned pale. "I could forgive a great deal in a sick man, but never this." Without another glance at anyone, he went out.

"How could you?" Razumihin said, shaking his head.

"Let me alone, all of you!" Raskolnikov cried. "I am not afraid of you! I am not afraid of anyone. Get away from me! I want to be alone!"

"Come along," said Zossimov, nodding to Razumihin.

"But we can't leave him like this!"

"Come along," Zossimov insisted, and he went out. Razumihin ran to catch up with him.

"It might be worse not to obey him," Zossimov said on the stairs. "He must not be excited."

"What's the matter with him?"

"You know, he has got something on his mind! Some idea is weighing on him," said Zossimov. "Have you noticed that he takes no interest in anything? There is, however, one point on which he seems excited—that's the murder."

"Yes, I noticed that, too. He seems interested and frightened. It gave him a shock on the day he was ill in the police office. He fainted."

Meanwhile Raskolnikov, left alone in his empty room, turned his body to the wall.

6 The Death of Marmeladov

When Raskolnikov got up, he began dressing in the clothes Razumihin had brought him. Strange to say, he seemed to have become perfectly calm. "Today, today," he muttered to himself.

When he had dressed, he noticed 25 rubles lying on the table. He put them in his pocket. He also took some copper change from the 10 rubles Razumihin had spent on clothes. Then he went out.

It was nearly eight o'clock. The sun was setting. It was as hot as before, and he breathed in the dusty, city air. A wild energy gleamed in his feverish eyes. He did not know where he was going. He had only one thought: "All *this* must be ended today."

Raskolnikov walked straight to a bridge. He leaned both elbows on the rail and stared into the distance. He suddenly felt much weaker and longed to lie down somewhere. He looked at the water for a long time. He was thinking about putting an end to it all. Then, suddenly, he felt disgusted.

"No, that's hateful. Water . . . it's not good enough," he muttered to himself. "No use to wait. What about the police office? Shall I tell them or not? The police office is open until ten o'clock.

41

"Very well, then," he said. His mind was made up. He walked away from the bridge and went in the direction of the police office. His heart felt empty. He did not want to think.

Raskolnikov walked on, turning into a side street, going two streets out of his way. He moved along, looking at the ground. Suddenly someone seemed to whisper in his ear. He lifted his head and saw that he was standing at the very gate of *the* house. He had not been near it since *that* evening.

Something drew him on. He went into the house and began climbing the familiar stairway to the fourth floor. He was surprised to find the door of the flat wide open. There were men inside. He could hear voices. He had not expected that. After a moment he went in. The walls were bare, and there was no furniture. It seemed strange. Two workmen were papering the walls with new white paper covered with tiny purple flowers.

"What do you want?" one of the workmen asked.

"I want to rent a flat," Raskolnikov said.

"At night is not the time to come looking at rooms."

"The floors have been washed. Will they be painted?" Raskolnikov went on. "Is there no blood?"

"What blood?"

"Why, the old woman and her sister were murdered here. There was a perfect pool there."

"But who are you?" the workman cried, uneasy.

"You want to know? Come to the police station then."

The workmen looked at him in amazement. Raskolnikov went out. He went slowly down the stairs.

"Shall I go there or not?" thought Raskolnikov, standing in the street. He looked about as if wanting an answer from someone. But no sound came. At the end of the street in the evening dusk he saw a crowd and heard shouts. He went up to the crowd.

A fancy carriage stood in the middle of the road. It was hitched to a pair of spirited horses. A policeman held a lantern shining on something on the ground. The coachman kept repeating, "What an accident! Good Lord, what an accident!"

Raskolnikov pushed his way in. On the ground lay a man who had been run over. He had been knocked out. Blood was flowing from his head. His face was crushed.

"I was not going fast!" wailed the coachman. "He was drunk. He fell straight under the horses' feet!"

Meanwhile, Raskolnikov had squeezed in and bent closer over the injured man. He recognized him.

"I know him! I know him!" he shouted, pushing to the front. "He's a government clerk no longer in the service. It is Marmeladov. He lives close by. Make haste for a doctor! I will pay, see?" He pulled money out of his pocket and showed it to the policeman.

Raskolnikov gave his own name and address. He begged the police to take Marmeladov to the man's lodging at once.

"Just here, three houses away. He was going home, no doubt, drunk. I know him. He has a family there. There is sure to be a doctor in the house. I'll pay, I'll pay!" They raised the injured man and began carrying him. Raskolnikov walked behind, carefully holding Marmeladov's head and showing the way.

Katerina Ivanovna was in her little room, talking to her oldest child and coughing. She seemed to have grown even thinner, and the flush on her face was brighter than ever. "You wouldn't believe what a happy life I once had," she was saying. "Now that drunkard has brought me to ruin. Oh, dear. What's this?" she cried, noticing a crowd in the hall. "What are they bringing? Mercy on us!"

"Where are we to put him?" asked the policeman when Marmeladov had been carried in.

"Put him on the sofa," Raskolnikov said.

"Run over in the road! Drunk!" someone shouted.

Katerina Ivanovna turned white. She gasped for breath. The children began crying. Raskolnikov went to Katerina.

"He was crossing the road and was run over by a carriage," he said. "I told them to bring him here. I've been here already. Do you remember me? Be calm. I'll pay."

Katerina rushed to her husband. She placed a pillow under his head and began examining him.

"I've sent for a doctor," Raskolnikov told Katerina. "Don't worry. I'll pay."

Raskolnikov found a towel and wet it. He began washing the blood off Marmeladov's face.

Katerina turned to her oldest child. "Run to Sonia. Hurry. Tell her that her father has been run over. Tell her to come."

The room had become crowded with people. Katerina turned to them. "You might let him die in peace, at least," she shouted. "Get away."

At that instant the dying man came to and groaned. Katerina ran to him. Blood oozed out of the corners of his mouth. Katerina looked at him with a sad but stern face. Tears fell from her eyes.

At that moment a young girl made her way through the crowd. She was dressed in a ragged kind of cheap finery. She wore a tight, bright silk dress and straw hat with a flame-colored feather. Under the hat was a pale, frightened little face. Sonia was a small, thin girl of 18 with fair hair, and wonderful blue eyes.

"Who's that? Who's that?" Marmeladov gasped. He saw his daughter in her cheap clothing, and his face showed pain.

"Sonia! Daughter! Forgive me!" he cried. Sonia gave a faint cry. She ran to him and held him. He died in her arms.

"He got what he wanted," Katerina Ivanovna cried, seeing her husband's dead body. "Well, what's to be done now? How am I to bury him?"

"Katerina Ivanovna," Raskolnikov said, "last week your husband told me all about his life. Believe me, he loved you in spite of his weakness for drinking. From that evening we became friends. Allow me to do something. Here are 25 rubles I will come again. I shall, perhaps, come tomorrow."

On the way out, Raskolnikov passed the policeman.

"You are spattered with blood," the policeman noted.

Raskolnikov looked at the fresh stains on his waistcoat. "Yes, I'm covered with blood," he said in a strange tone. Then he smiled, nodded, and went downstairs.

He walked down slowly. He was filled with a new feeling of strength and of life. He felt like a man who had been sentenced to death but has just been pardoned.

"Wait, wait!" a voice called. Raskolnikov turned. It was one of Marmeladov's children. "Sister Sonia sent me," she cried. "Mamma sent me, too." She threw her arms, thin as sticks, around his neck. "Tell me, what is your name and where do you live?"

Raskolnikov felt a great joy looking at her. "My name is Raskolnikov. Pray for me sometimes."

"I'll pray for you all the rest of my life," the little girl declared. She hugged him warmly.

Raskolnikov told her his address and promised to come the next day. It was past ten o'clock when he came onto the street.

"Enough," he said. "I'm done with imaginary terrors. I believe my illness is over. Life is real! Haven't I lived just now? My life has not yet died with that old woman!"

He easily found Razumihin. Razumihin was at his little party, in the company of 15 people.

"I can't come in," Raskolnikov said. "I am too weak. And so good evening. Come and see me tomorrow."

"I'll see you home," Razumihin said. "I must. You are weak."

On the way to Raskolnikov's room, Razumihin spoke freely. "Do you know what Zossimov whispered to me when we were coming out? Zossimov told me to get you to talk and to tell him about it afterwards. He's got an idea in his head that you are mad or close to it. With your strange interest in the recent murders and with your fainting in the police station, an idea is being hatched in his brain. Porfiry is at the bottom of it. He took advantage of your fainting at the police station. But it's all cleared up."

Raskolnikov listened eagerly. Razumihin had been drinking and was talking too freely.

"I fainted because it was so stuffy and because of the smell of the paint," said Raskolnikov.

For half a minute both were silent.

"Look! What's that?" Raskolnikov cried suddenly.

"What is it?"

"Don't you see? A light in my room, through the crack."

When they reached the door, they heard voices. Raskolnikov opened the door. He stood there, shocked.

His mother and sister were sitting on his sofa. They had been waiting an hour and a half for him. He had been told they were coming, yet he had forgotten all about them.

A cry of joy greeted Raskolnikov. Both women rushed to him. But he stood like a dead man. He did not lift his arms to hug them. His mother and sister held him, kissed him, laughed and cried. He took a step and fell to the ground, fainting.

Razumihin ran into the room. He lifted the sick man in his strong arms and in a moment had him on the sofa.

"He will be all right," Razumihin cried. "He has been sick, but he is much better."

The mother and sister gave Razumihin a look of thanks.

7 Family Matters

Pulcheria and Dounia held Raskolnikov by the hand. Pulcheria began to cry. Dounia was pale.

"Go home—with him," Raskolnikov said in a broken voice. He pointed to Razumihin. "Good-bye until tomorrow."

"I won't leave you like this," Pulcheria cried.

"Come, mamma, we are upsetting him," Dounia said.

"Wait," Raskolnikov said suddenly. "Have you seen Luzhin?"

"No, but he knows of our arrival," said Pulcheria. "We have heard, son, that he was so kind as to visit you."

"Yes, he was so kind. Dounia, I promised Luzhin I'd throw him down the stairs. I told him to go to hell."

"What are you saying?" Pulcheria said in alarm.

"Dounia," Raskolnikov continued, "I don't want that marriage. You must refuse Luzhin."

"Brother, think what you are saying!" Dounia cried. Then she stopped. "You are ill. You are not fit to talk now."

"You think I don't know what I say? No, you are marrying Luzhin for *my* sake. But I won't accept the sacrifice. Write a letter to him tomorrow. Refuse him."

"I can't do that," Dounia cried. "What right have you to say this?"

"He is raving," Razumihin said, "or how would he dare? Tomorrow all this nonsense will be over. He did get angry with Luzhin. And Luzhin got angry, too. He drove him away."

"Good-bye until tomorrow, brother," Dounia said. "Let us go, mother."

"Do you hear, sister?" Raskolnikov called after them. "I am not crazy. This marriage is wrong. It's me or Luzhin!"

Then Raskolnikov lay down on the sofa and turned toward the wall.

Pulcheria did not want to leave her son. Razumihin convinced her that she must go. He offered to see both women home. He promised to bring the doctor, Zossimov, to care for Raskolnikov during the night. Razumihin held Pulcheria's hands. He held Dounia's hands. He wanted to help them. If they had told him to leap headfirst off the staircase, he would have done it.

Razumihin stared at Dounia, a light glowing in his eyes. "I am his friend," he cried, "and therefore I am your friend, too."

"Here is your lodging," Razumihin said at last. He looked up at the building. "For this alone, Raskolnikov was right in driving Luzhin away. How dare he put you up in such a place? Luzhin is a scoundrel."

"Excuse me, sir," Pulcheria began. "You are forgetting . . . "

"Yes, yes, you are right," Razumihin apologized. "I did forget myself. I am sorry. But you can't be angry with me for speaking honestly. We all saw when he came to visit. That man is not our sort! Well, goodnight. Lock yourselves in."

"Good heavens, Dounia, what is going to happen?" said Pulcheria once they were in their room.

"Don't worry, mother," said Dounia, taking off her hat and cape. "God has sent this gentleman to help us."

Dounia began walking up and down, her arms folded. It was not surprising that Razumihin had liked her so much. Dounia was a very attractive woman. She was tall and strong, yet graceful. She looked quite a bit like her brother. Her hair was dark brown, a little lighter than her brother's. There was a proud light in her black eyes and, at times, a look of great kindness. Her face was more serious than gay, but a smile could light it up. Some might call her really beautiful. It was no wonder that a warm, open, simple-hearted man like Razumihin should lose his head over her.

At nine o'clock the next morning, Razumihin returned to the mother and sister. He had dressed carefully. He had only one suit, but he had brushed it. He had washed his hair and scrubbed his neck and hands. When he arrived, both women were waiting.

Pulcheria said that she had something to talk over with him before they saw Raskolnikov again. She began to ask questions about her son.

Razumihin answered questions about the last years of Raskolnikov's life. He told them about the illness. He did leave out some things, including the trip to the police station.

"He seems so very different," Pulcheria said.

"What am I to tell you?" said Razumihin. "I have known him for a year and a half. He is gloomy and proud. He has a noble nature and a kind heart. He does not like showing his feelings. Sometimes he can be very cold. It is as though he had two characters. He sets himself apart from other people. He says he is too busy to do something, and yet he lies in bed doing nothing. He thinks very highly of himself. Perhaps he is right. I think your arrival will do him some good."

"Oh, I hope so," cried Pulcheria. Then she began to speak of a letter that had arrived from Luzhin. "Very early this morning we got a note from Luzhin. One thing in it worries me. Tell us your opinion."

Razumihin opened the note and read as follows:

"Dear Madam Pulcheria Raskolnikov, I am sorry I was not able to meet you at the station. I should like to visit your lodgings at eight o'clock tomorrow evening. I ask that your son not be present at our meeting. He insulted me when I visited him. Although he has been ill, I have learned he was well enough to leave his lodgings. In fact, he went to the home of a drunken man who was run over and killed by a carriage. Your son did, I understand, give 25 rubles to a young woman of questionable behavior. This surprised me, knowing how hard it was for you to raise that money. I send my deepest respect to your daughter. Your humble servant, P. Luzhin"

"What am I to do, Razumihin?" began Pulcheria, almost weeping. "How can I ask my son not to come here?"

"Do whatever Dounia wishes," Razumihin answered.

"She says that her brother must be here at eight o'clock. She says they must meet. But I don't understand about that drunkard who died and the young woman. How could he have given her all the money?"

"He has not been himself," Razumihin said.

"The best thing, Mother, would be for us to go to him ourselves," Dounia said.

The women followed Razumihin to Raskolnikov's

flat. Pulcheria was pale and very nervous about the meeting. They found Zossimov with Raskolnikov.

"He is well, quite well!" the doctor said cheerfully as they came in.

Raskolnikov was fully dressed and carefully washed and combed, as he had not been for some time. He was really much better, but he was still pale and serious. He gave his mother and sister a kiss of welcome. This cheered Pulcheria.

He talked with them. Indeed, he did seem better. He even told them about happening upon the carriage accident.

"A man, a clerk, had been run over. I got spattered by blood helping to carry him to his lodging. And, Mamma, I did an unforgivable thing. I was so upset. I gave away the money you sent me . . . to his wife for the funeral. They were so poor. I had no right to do it. But perhaps you might have done the same if you had seen them. I beg your forgiveness, Mother."

"That is all right, son," Pulcheria said. "I am sure everything you do is very good."

"Don't be too sure," he answered with a twisted smile.

Then he turned to his sister. "Listen, Dounia," he began seriously. "I beg your pardon for yesterday. But I consider it my duty to tell you again how I feel. It is either me or Luzhin. If you marry Luzhin, I will no longer look on you as a sister!"

"Brother, you are wrong," said Dounia. "You think that I am sacrificing myself to Luzhin for others. That is not the case. I am simply marrying for my own sake because things are hard for me. I shall be glad if this brings some good to my family, of course."

"You are lying," said Raskolnikov. "You cannot respect Luzhin. I have seen him and talked with him. So you are selling yourself for money."

"It is not true. I am not lying. Why are you so hard on me? You are no hero. Why must I be one? If I ruin anyone, it is only myself. I am not committing a murder. Why do you look at me like that? Why are you so pale? What is the matter?"

"Good heavens! You have made him faint!" cried Pulcheria.

"No, no. I am all right," Raskolnikov said.

"Give him the letter," Dounia said to her mother.

With trembling hands, Pulcheria handed Raskolnikov the letter from Luzhin. He read it twice. Then he handed it back.

"He lies about me," Raskolnikov said. "I gave money to a widow to pay for a funeral, not to the daughter. I see he is trying to make trouble between us."

"What will you do, son?" asked Pulcheria. "You see that Luzhin writes that you are not to be with us this evening."

"I will do what you think best," Raskolnikov answered.

"Dounia has already decided. She wants you to come to the meeting."

"I want you to be with us as well," Dounia said, turning to Razumihin.

"So be it," said Pulcheria. "I feel better. I do not like lies and secrets between us. Luzhin may be angry or not!"

At that moment the door opened, and a young girl walked into the room. She looked around shyly. Everyone in the room turned toward her with surprise. It was Sonia Marmeladov. Today she was a very plainly dressed young girl. She looked very young, almost like a child. She had a somewhat frightened-looking face. She could not have been called pretty, but she had kindly, clear blue eyes. Sonia had not expected to find the room full of people. She looked around in surprise.

"I did not expect you," Raskolnikov said. "Come in. Please sit down." He showed Sonia a chair between his mother and sister.

Sonia sat down, shaking a bit. She looked at the women. "I . . . I . . . have come for one minute. Forgive me for bothering you. I come from Katerina Ivanovna. She told me to ask you to be at the service . . . in the morning . . ." Sonia stammered.

"I will try, certainly," said Raskolnikov.

Sonia took a hurried, frightened look at the two women.

"Mother," Raskolnikov said firmly, "this is Sonia Marmeladov. She is the daughter of poor Mr. Marmeladov who was run over yesterday. I was just telling you about him."

"Katerina begs you to do us the honor of being in the church for the service tomorrow," Sonia explained. "She will give a little funeral lunch. She told me to thank you for helping us yesterday. If not for you, we would have nothing for the funeral." Sonia's lips and chin began to tremble. She looked around the tiny room.

"Sonia, why do you look at my room like that?"

"You gave us everything yesterday," she said quietly. She had noted Raskolnikov's poor surroundings.

A silence followed.

"We must go," said Pulcheria. "We will see you tonight then," she said to Raskolnikov and Razumihin.

As she left, Dounia gave Sonia a polite, friendly bow. Sonia, confused, returned a frightened little curtsy. She looked very uncomfortable.

In the streets, Pulcheria said to Dounia, "I am very much afraid of that young woman."

"Why, mother?" asked Dounia.

"I have a feeling that she is a cause of his trouble."

"Nothing of the sort!" cried Dounia. "Why he only just met her the evening before."

"Well," said Pulcheria, "you will see."

8 A Visit to Porfiry

Sonia still sat quietly in her chair. Raskolnikov began talking to Razumihin.

"You know that . . . what's his name . . . Porfiry?"

"I should think so," Razumihin answered. "He is my uncle."

"Is he not in charge of that case . . . you know, the murder? You were speaking of it yesterday."

"Yes. Why?" Razumihin's eyes opened wide.

"He wanted to talk to people who had pawned things. I left some items there—a ring my sister gave me, my father's silver watch. I do not want to lose them, especially the watch. It is the only thing of Father's left to us. Do you think I should go to Porfiry? He might be able to settle the matter quickly."

"Certainly," Razumihin shouted in excitement. "Well, how glad I am. Let us go at once. He will be very glad to meet you. I have talked of you at different times. So you knew the old woman? So that's it. Everything is turning out fine."

"I must go now," Sonia interrupted, looking uncomfortable.

"Yes, we must go, too," said Raskolnikov. "I will come to see you today, Sonia. Where do you live?"

Sonia gave him her address, flushing as she did so. They all went out together.

Sonia was very glad to get away. She walked along looking at the ground, thinking about the meeting. She did not notice the stranger following her. The gentleman had watched her taking leave of Raskolnikov. He had noted the house and the address. And now he followed her.

He was a man of about 50. He was rather tall and thickly set. He wore good clothes and carried a handsome cane, which he tapped on the sidewalk at each step. His eyes were blue and had a cold look.

When Sonia turned in at her gate, the stranger stopped. Then he went on to the lodging next door. He turned back to Sonia and smiled. "You live here? Then we are neighbors. I only came to town the day before yesterday. Good-bye for now."

Sonia did not answer. She opened the door and slipped in. She felt, for some reason, uneasy.

On the way to Porfiry's, Razumihin was very excited. "I didn't know you pawned some things at the old woman's. That is why, in your fever, you spoke of some rings or chains. Yes. It's all clear now. Here it is, this gray house," Razumihin continued.

"My heart is beating," Raskolnikov thought. "The most important thing: does Porfiry know I stopped at the old hag's flat yesterday and asked about the blood?"

"I say, brother," Raskolnikov said to Razumihin, changing the subject. "I notice that you have been quite excited all day. And you blushed when you were invited to my sister's this evening. Why, you are blushing again. And you have cleaned your nails and fixed up your hair. Why, you Romeo!"

Raskolnikov laughed as if he could not stop. So laughing, they entered Porfiry's flat. This is what Raskolnikov wanted. They could be heard laughing as they came in.

"This is my friend, Raskolnikov," Razumihin said. "He wanted to meet you. Also, he has a little matter of business."

Porfiry was wearing a dressing gown and slippers. He was a short, round man. His face was plump and clean-shaven. His look might have been called kindly, except for sharp eyes that shone under white, blinking eyelashes. Those eyes did not match his soft, round figure.

Porfiry asked Raskolnikov to sit down. He waited for his visitor to explain his business. In brief, clear words, Raskolnikov explained. He said that he had pawned some items that he wanted to claim. He did not have the money to buy them back now, but he wanted to make clear that they were his. He would, he said, be back for them. Porfiry did not once take his eyes off Raskolnikov.

"He knows," flashed through Raskolnikov's mind.

"Your things will not be lost," Porfiry said coldly. "I have been expecting you here for some time. Your things, the ring and the watch, were wrapped up together. On the paper your name was written in pencil with the date you left them with her."

"How well you remember things!" Raskolnikov said. "There must have been many items left there."

"We know all who had items left with her. You are the only one who hadn't yet come forward," said Porfiry.

"I haven't been well."

"I heard that, too. I heard, indeed, that you were very upset about something. You look pale still."

"No, I am quite well now," Raskolnikov snapped. He was getting angry and he could not hide it. "Shall my anger give me away?" he wondered. "Why is he torturing me?"

"But why did you go out when you were ill?" Porfiry asked. "I understand you were at the lodgings of a man who had been run over."

"I was tired of everyone fussing over me. I ran away to get away from them. But, this must all be boring you, Inspector Porfiry."

"Oh, no. Not a bit. If only you knew how you interest me! I am really glad you have come forward at last."

Porfiry rose to get some tea. Raskolnikov's thoughts were in a whirl. He began shaking with anger. "Don't play with me like a dog," he thought. "Perhaps I won't allow it! I shall get up and throw the whole truth in your ugly face!" He could hardly breathe. "But what if this is only my imagination? What if he does not suspect at all? There are no facts. He is just trying to catch me."

Porfiry returned with the tea. He seemed friendlier.

"Remember last night, at your party?" he said to Razumihin. "We were talking about crime. We were discussing what it was that made criminals turn to crime. The conversation made me remember an article you once wrote, Raskolnikov. I read it with interest two months ago in the *Periodical Review.*"

"My article? The *Periodical Review?*" Raskolnikov asked, surprised. "I certainly did write an article six months ago when I left the university. I did not know it was printed. I wrote about the way a criminal thinks before and after a crime."

"Yes, and you wrote that a crime is always accompanied by an illness. You also suggested that certain persons have a right to commit crimes, that the law is not for them."

"What do you mean, a right to commit crimes?" exclaimed Razumihin. "Do you mean because they have led hard lives?"

"No," answered Porfiry. "In his article all men are divided into 'ordinary' and 'extraordinary.' Ordinary men have to obey the law. But extraordinary men have a right to commit any crime, to break the law, just because they are extraordinary. That was your idea, if I am not wrong?"

"Yes, that is almost correct. However, I do not say that extraordinary people must commit crimes. I do say to consider this. What if great discoveries in science could not have been made without sacrificing the lives of a few? Then the scientists would have had the right, the duty, to get rid of those people who stood in their way. Why, all great leaders and lawmakers were criminals. In making a new law, they broke an old one."

"But tell me, how do we tell these extraordinary people from the ordinary ones?" Porfiry asked. "Are there many of these extraordinary people who have the right to kill?"

"People with new ideas are extremely few in number." Raskolnikov said.

"What if some young man fancies himself to be extraordinary? What if he needs money for one of his extraordinary plans and tries to get it? Do you see?"

"Then you have but to catch the thief."

"What of his conscience? Does he ever feel guilty for his crime?" Porfiry asked.

"If he has a conscience, he will suffer. That will be his punishment. Pain and suffering always come to those of large intelligence and a deep heart. The really great men must, I think, have great sadness on earth," Raskolnikov added dreamily. He raised his eyes and picked up his cap.

"So could you bring yourself to rob and murder to overcome something that stood in your way?" Porfiry asked.

"If I did, I certainly should not tell you," Raskolnikov answered. He looked firmly at Porfiry.

"Are you going already?" Porfiry asked. He held out his hand. "Very, very glad to meet you. Come back tomorrow. We will see that you get your things back. We will have a talk."

"You want to question me officially?" Raskolnikov asked.

"Oh, that is not necessary for the present. By the way, you went up to the pawnbroker's flat to leave your items? When you went up it was evening? Past seven, wasn't it?"

"Yes," answered Raskolnikov.

"Then, when you went upstairs, didn't you see a flat that stood open on the second story? Two workmen were painting there. Didn't you notice them?"

"Painters? No, I didn't see them." He answered slowly. Was this some trap? "I remember that someone was moving out of a flat across from Alyona Ivanovna's. But painters—I don't remember any painters." He had beaten the trap now, and felt pleased.

"What do you mean?" Razumihin shouted. "It was on the day of the murder that the painters were at work. Raskolnikov was there three days before! What are you asking?"

"Oh! I am wrong," Porfiry slapped himself on the forehead. He turned to Raskolnikov as if to apologize. "It would be very helpful if someone had been there and perhaps could have told us something."

Porfiry saw them to the door. Once outside, Raskolnikov and Razumihin did not say a word.

By the time Raskolnikov got home, his hair was soaked with sweat and he was breathing heavily. He went up the stairs, walked into his unlocked room, and at once fastened the latch. Then, in terror, he rushed about his flat. He was looking for some evidence that might prove him a murderer.

Then he sank down. "Ah, how I hate the old woman now! I feel I should kill her again if she came to life! Poor Lizaveta! Why did she come in? Why is it I never think of her? It is as though I hadn't killed her. Lizaveta! Sonia! Poor gentle things, with gentle eyes. They give up everything. Sonia! Gentle Sonia!"

He fell into a deep sleep. The old woman was before him. She was shaking with laughter. He was overcome with anger and began hitting her on the head with all his force. He tried to scream and woke up.

He drew a deep breath. But his dream seemed strangely to stay with him.

Then his door was flung open. A man whom he had never seen stood in the doorway watching him.

Raskolnikov closed his eyes again. "Is it still a dream?" he wondered. He raised his eyelids. The stranger was still watching him. He came into the room and sat down. He leaned his hands on his cane. A big fly buzzed against the windowpane. Raskolnikov suddenly sat up.

"Come, tell me what you want."

"I knew you were not asleep." The stranger laughed. "I am Svidrigailov."

9 Dounia's Suitors

"Can this still be a dream?" Raskolnikov thought again.

He looked carefully at the visitor. "Svidrigailov! It can't be!" he said, confused.

"I've come to see you for two reasons," the man said. "In the first place, I wanted to meet you. I have heard interesting things about you. Second, I hope that you will arrange a meeting with your sister. Without your help, she probably will not let me come near her. She hates me. With your help, I think I . . ."

"You think wrongly," interrupted Raskolnikov.

"Tell me, Raskolnikov, what was it that I did that was so wrong? What crime did I commit? That I went after a young girl in my own house? I am human. I can fall in love. The question is, am I a monster, or am I, myself, a victim? I asked Dounia to run off with me to America or Switzerland. I was the slave of passion. Why, I was probably doing more harm to myself than to anyone!"

"But that is not the point," said Raskolnikov. "It's simply that whether you are right or wrong, we dislike you. We don't want to have anything to do with you. We show you the door!"

"Raskolnikov, there would have been no problem, if my wife had not caught me pleading with your sister in the garden."

"Your wife! I understand you've gotten rid of her."

"I had nothing to do with her death. The doctor said she had a stroke. Perhaps it was brought on by bathing right after a heavy dinner. Why, my wife and I hardly ever fought. I only beat her twice in all the years we were married."

"Why do you tell me all this?" asked Raskolnikov.

"I need someone to talk to," said Svidrigailov. "And Raskolnikov, you seem to be a rather strange person yourself. I believe we have much in common. We are birds of a feather."

"Why have you paid me this visit?" Raskolnikov said angrily.

"Your sister is going to be married to Mr. Luzhin?"

"Don't say my sister's name! How dare you say her name?"

"But I am sure you must have formed your own opinion of this Luzhin. He is not good enough for Dounia. I believe Dounia is sacrificing herself for the sake of her family. Surely you would be happy if this match could be broken off."

"You are only interested in your own gains," Raskolnikov said.

"I am no longer in love with your sister. In fact, I wonder now if I ever was. I just want you to help me meet with her. I want to explain that Luzhin will harm her. I want to beg her pardon for the troubles I have caused her. I want to offer her 10,000 rubles. This would help her break with Luzhin."

"You are certainly crazy," cried Raskolnikov.

"I only want to make up for any harm I might have done Dounia. There is nothing in it for myself. In fact, I have plans to marry another young lady. Please, tell Dounia of my offer."

"No, I won't," said Raskolnikov.

"In that case, I will have to try to see her myself. Oh yes, tell your sister one thing for me. My wife remembered her in her will. She left her 3,000 rubles. She was sorry for the trouble we caused her. Dounia will receive the money in two or three weeks. Tell her. Well, I will be nearby."

As he went out, Svidrigailov met Razumihin coming in. It was nearly eight o'clock. Razumihin and Raskolnikov had to hurry to the meeting with Luzhin.

"Who was that?" asked Razumihin when they were in the street.

"It was Svidrigailov. My sister worked for him in his house. He insulted her with his attentions. He tried to force himself on her. She was thrown out by his wife. Afterward, the wife begged Dounia's forgiveness. She died suddenly. I don't know why I am afraid of that man. He came here right after his wife's funeral. He is very strange, and he means to do something. We must guard Dounia from him."

"If he means harm, we will guard her!" Razumihin said.

"At first I thought it might all be a dream. I thought I imagined his visit. Perhaps I really am mad and everything that happens these days is only imagination."

"Oh, Raskolnikov, you have been upset again. Now let me tell you what I have decided about my uncle Porfiry. I have decided we should not bother ourselves about his ideas. You didn't do anything wrong. What do we care what he thinks? We shall have a laugh at him afterward!"

Raskolnikov looked at Razumihin. For the first time he wondered what Razumihin would think if he knew the truth.

In the hall they met Luzhin. He had arrived exactly at eight. The three went in without looking at one another. Luzhin bowed to the women. He looked, however, a little annoyed.

Pulcheria had them all sit down at a round table where a teapot was boiling. A silence fell. Luzhin pulled out a perfumed handkerchief and blew his nose. He acted hurt that his request had been ignored, and that Raskolnikov and Razumihin were present.

"You had a pleasant journey?" he said to Dounia at last.

"It was fine," she answered. "Mother got a bit tired traveling so long."

"Well, Mother Russia is a large country. I am sorry I was unable to meet you yesterday."

"Well, Razumihin has made things easier for us," declared Pulcheria. "This is Razumihin," she said as introduction.

"I had the pleasure yesterday," said Luzhin, frowning.

Again all was silent.

"Did you know that Mr. Svidrigailov has come to St. Petersburg?" Luzhin said at last.

"Here?" cried Dounia in alarm.

"I imagine he will leave you alone," said Luzhin.

"Oh, you don't know what a fright that gives me," Pulcheria cried. "He is a terrible man. I am sure he was the cause of his own wife's death!"

"I have heard that he has done some terrible things in his life," said Luzhin. "I understand that his wife had gotten him out of trouble with the law a few times."

"Luzhin, say no more about Mr. Svidrigailov," Dounia said. "It makes me miserable."

"He has just been to see me," said Raskolnikov. It was the first time he had spoken. "He was quite friendly. He asked me to arrange a meeting with you,

Dounia. He has something to speak with you about. He also said that his wife left you 3,000 rubles in her will."

" Pray for her soul!" cried Pulcheria.

"What else did he say?" asked Dounia.

"I will tell you later." Raskolnikov stopped talking and turned to his tea.

Luzhin looked at his watch. "I have a business meeting and must leave."

"Don't go," said Dounia. "You wrote that you wanted to meet with us."

"Yes, but, just as your brother cannot discuss his conversation with Mr. Svidrigailov in front of me, so I cannot speak freely in the presence of others. You paid no attention to my request that we meet without him."

"I am aware that I did not honor your request," said Dounia. "You wrote that you had been insulted by my brother. I think this must be explained. If my brother really has insulted you, then he should apologize. This is important. I must find out who is really at fault. If it comes to it, I must choose between my brother and you."

Luzhin became angry at this statement. "Love for your future husband should be more important than love for your brother. My wishes were not met concerning this meeting!"

"You seem to think you can command us to do things, Luzhin," said Pulcheria. "We gave up everything to come here as you asked. Now we rely on you."

"That is not quite true, now that Svidrigailov's wife has left you money," Luzhin said. And who knows what kind of offer Svidrigailov has for you Dounia!"

"Good heavens!" cried Pulcheria at the insult.

Razumihin could not sit still in his chair.

"Well, sister, see what he is like?" said Raskolnikov.

"I am ashamed of myself, brother," said Dounia. "Luzhin, go away." She turned to him white with anger.

Luzhin had not expected such an ending. His lips shook. "Dounia, if I go out this door now, I will never return!"

Dounia sprang from her seat. "I don't want you to come back!"

"Do you think I would give my daughter to a man like you?" cried Pulcheria. "Go away!"

"I am going. But one last word," he said. He could hardly control himself. "I was kind enough to pay no attention to the gossip about you, Dounia. I was willing to marry you anyway."

"Does this fellow want his head smashed?" cried Razumihin, jumping up.

"Not a word!" cried Raskolnikov, holding Razumihin back. Then he went close up to Luzhin. "Kindly leave the room!" he said quietly. "And not a word more or—"

Luzhin glared at them for some seconds. His face was pale and he shook with anger. Then he turned and went out. Rarely has any man hated anyone as he hated Raskolnikov. But as Luzhin went downstairs, he had not given up. He felt that all might be set right with Dounia again.

10 Sonia

Luzhin went away very angry. His plans had been ruined. He had never thought that two helpless women could escape from his control. For many years Luzhin had dreamed of finding a girl like Dounia—someone good, poor (she must be poor), young, pretty, well-educated. He had dreamed of someone who would depend on him and do his bidding. Dounia was perfect. He had to get Dounia back. And he had to settle things with Raskolnikov. Raskolnikov was the cause of all the trouble!

"Oh, I am to blame!" Dounia walked up and down in her room. "I was tempted by his money. I had no idea he was such a terrible man."

"God has delivered us!" cried Pulcheria.

They were happy that Luzhin was gone. Razumihin did not dare let his joy show yet. But he felt that anything might happen now! Only Raskolnikov did not seem happy.

"What did Svidrigailov say to you?" Dounia asked him.

"He wants to give you 10,000 rubles, and he wants to see you."

"What did you tell him?" asked Dounia.

"At first I said I would not take any message to you. Then he said he is over his feelings for you. He said he is sorry for the trouble he caused. He said he did not want you to marry Luzhin. I thought he was very strange. One might almost think he was crazy. Of course, I refused his money."

Dounia stood thinking about Svidrigailov's offer. "He has some terrible plan," she whispered at last.

"I will watch out for you," said Razumihin. "Your brother has said, 'Take care of my sister,' and I will."

Suddenly Raskolnikov rose to leave.

"Where are you going?" cried his mother.

"It would be better for us to part for a time. I feel ill. I am not at peace. Leave me alone. Whatever may come to me, I want to be alone. If you love me, give me up. Good-bye."

"Good God!" cried Pulcheria. "Don't go like this!"

Raskolnikov turned and ran out of the room. Razumihin went after him. He found Raskolnikov waiting for him at the end of the hall.

"I knew that you would come after me," said Rasklolnikov. "Go back to them. Be with them. Perhaps I will come back—if I can. Good-bye."

"But where are you going? What are you doing?" Razumihin cried.

"Once and for all, I have nothing to tell you. Don't come to see me. Leave me, but *don't leave them*. Do you understand?"

It was dark in the hall. They were standing near a dim lamp. For a minute, they stood looking at each other. Razumihin would remember that minute all his life. Raskolnikov's eyes burned into his soul. Suddenly Razumihin jumped. Something strange passed between them—some awful, terrible idea. Razumihin turned pale.

"Do you understand now?" said Raskolnikov. "Go back to them," he said suddenly. He turned and went out of the house.

Razumihin went back to the women. He said he was sure Raskolnikov would be back. He promised he would watch over him. He said he would visit them every day. From that evening Razumihin began caring for them like a son and a brother.

Raskolnikov went straight to Sonia's lodging.

"Good heavens!" Sonia cried weakly when Raskolnikov came to her room.

Raskolnikov looked about rapidly. Sonia's room looked much like a barn. There was scarcely any furniture. Old, yellow wallpaper had turned black at the corners.

"I might not see you after this," said Raskolnikov. "I've come to say one thing. But why are you standing? Sit down." Raskolnikov took Sonia's hand. "How thin you are," he said. "What will happen to you now, Sonia? Who will take care of Katerina and the children?"

"I don't know. They owe rent money. I heard that the landlady wants to get rid of them. I want to help them. But, you know, sometimes I can be quite cruel to them. Only last week, only a week before his death, I was so cruel."

"You were cruel?"

"Yes. I went to see them. 'Read to me,' my father said. 'My head hurts.' And I said, 'I can't stay.' I just didn't want to read. I had come to show Katerina some collars that Lizaveta the peddler sold me. I should have read to my father!"

"Did you know Lizaveta, the peddler?"

"Yes, did you know her?" Sonia asked in surprise.

"Katerina is very sick. She will soon die," said Raskolnikov after a pause. He did not answer her question.

"Oh no! No!"

"Then the children will depend on you," he said. "How will you support them? Perhaps the oldest girl can sell herself on the streets like you."

"No, no! It can't be!" Sonia cried as though she had been stabbed. "God would not allow it!"

"Perhaps there is no God," said Raskolnikov.

He paced up and down the room. At last he went to Sonia. His eyes glittered. All at once he bent down quickly and dropped to the ground. He kissed her foot. Sonia drew back from him as if he were mad.

"What are you doing to me?" she whispered, turning pale.

"I did not bow down to you. I bowed down to the suffering of all people," Raskolnikov said. "You are worthy of great honor."

"Why, I am dishonorable. Why do you say I am worthy of honor?"

"You have sinned, it is true. But you have also suffered."

There was a Bible on the table. Raskolnikov picked it up.

"Where did you get this?" he asked her.

"From Lizaveta. I asked her for it."

"Lizaveta! Strange!" he thought.

Everything about Sonia seemed stranger and more wonderful every moment.

"Were you friends with Lizaveta, Sonia?"

"Yes, she was good. We used to read together and talk. She was killed with an axe. She will see God."

"I came to speak of something," Raskolnikov said, frowning. He went to Sonia. She lifted her eyes to him.

"I left my family today," he said. "I have only you now. We have both sinned. Let us go our way together!"

"His eyes glitter as though he is mad," thought Sonia. "Go where?" she asked in alarm.

"How do I know? I only know it is the same road."

Sonia looked at him. She did not understand. She only knew he was very unhappy.

"I need you, Sonia. No one will understand but you. Haven't you done the same as me? You have done wrong. You, too, have destroyed a life—your own. It's all the same. If you stay alone, you will go out of your mind like me. I may come here again tomorrow. If I come tomorrow, I'll tell you who killed Lizaveta. Good-bye."

Sonia jumped. "Why, do you know who killed her?" she asked. She was cold with terror.

"I know and will tell you—only you. I have chosen you. I'm not coming to you to ask forgiveness, but simply to tell you. Good-bye. Tomorrow!"

He went out. Sonia looked at him as at a madman. She felt as if she, herself, were going crazy.

"Good heavens, how does he know who killed Lizaveta? What did those words mean?" *The idea* did not enter her head.

Sonia did not sleep well that night. She dreamed of Katerina and Lizaveta. And she dreamed of him— him with pale face and burning eyes, kissing her feet, weeping.

A door on the right divided Sonia's room from another room. It was a room that had stood empty. But now someone stayed there. All that time Mr. Svidrigailov had been standing, listening at the door of that room. When Raskolnikov went out, Svidrigailov stood still and thought a moment. Then he carried a chair to the door that led to Sonia's room.

The conversation he had heard had been very interesting. He had greatly enjoyed it. He moved the chair so that in the future he would not have to stand to listen. Tomorrow, for instance, he might listen in comfort.

11 Cat and Mouse

The next morning Raskolnikov went to the police station to see Porfiry. He was surprised that he was kept waiting. He was shaking. He was angry at himself for being afraid to see Porfiry. He hated that man, and he was afraid that his hatred might give him away. He forced himself to become calm and cold. He decided he would keep as silent as possible.

When he was called in, he found Porfiry alone in his office. Porfiry at once rose and closed the door. He met Raskolnikov with a cheerful air.

"Ah, my dear fellow! Come in. Sit down."

Raskolnikov sat down. Each man watched the other. When their eyes met, quick as lightning they looked away.

"I brought you this paper about my father's watch," said Raskolnikov.

"Yes, fine," said Porfiry. He took it and put it away. He began talking of other things. He was making simple, everyday conversation.

Raskolnikov interrupted him. "I believe you said yesterday you would like to question me about my business with the murdered woman?"

"Yes, yes. There is no hurry," said Porfiry. He walked about the room. His fat, round little figure looked strange. He looked like a ball rolling from one side to the other. "We have plenty of time. Do you smoke? Would you like a cigarette?"

Raskolnikov was determined not to fall into any trap. He would not be fooled by conversation. "Porfiry," he began, "yesterday you said you wanted to talk to me. I have come, and if you have anything to ask me, ask it. If not, let me go. I have no time to spare. I have to be at the funeral of a man who was run over." At once he was angry at himself for mentioning this. "I am sick of it all, do you hear? Kindly question me or let me go at once. If you must question me, do so in the proper way."

"Good heavens! What do you mean? What shall I question you about?" asked Porfiry. "Please don't get upset. I'm very glad you've come to see me at last. I look upon you simply as a visitor. Do sit down. Please do, or I shall think you are angry."

Raskolnikov sat down but still held his cap.

"Do put down your cap. Why not spend five minutes with a friend?" Porfiry went on. He began talking about his work, about other cases. He walked up and down about the room chatting and laughing. "But why are you so pale, Raskolnikov?" he asked. "Is the room stuffy? Shall I open a window?"

"Oh, don't trouble, please," cried Raskolnikov. He suddenly broke into a laugh. "Please don't trouble."

Then Raskolnikov got up. He stopped his laughter. "Porfiry," he began, speaking loudly. His legs shook and he could hardly stand. "I see clearly at last that you suspect me of murdering that old woman and her sister Lizaveta. Let me tell you for my part that I am sick of this. If you have a case against me, arrest me. But I will not let you play with me like a cat with a mouse." His eyes glowed with anger.

"Good heavens! What does it mean?" cried Porfiry. "My dear fellow, what is the matter with you? Some fresh air! And you must have some water. You're ill." Porfiry poured a glass of water for Raskolnikov. "Come, drink a little," he whispered. "It will do you good."

The round little man went on. "Now, I know you have been upset. I know more than that about you. I know how you went to take a flat at night when it was dark. I know how you asked to see the blood, so that the workmen did not know what to make of you. But you are going to drive yourself mad!"

Raskolnikov was hot all over. "How can it be? He knows about my visit to the flat then, and he tells me himself!"

"I've had cases like this before," Porfiry went on. "A man confessed to murder but it was all imagination. It was an illness. You should see a doctor, Raskolnikov. You are lightheaded. You were very sick when you went to the flat."

"Is he lying or not?" wondered Raskolnikov. "I was not sick," he said. "I knew what I was doing." He would spoil Porfiry's game. "I was quite myself, do you hear?"

"No, you have been ill. Your mother and sister are here now. You must take care of yourself for their sakes."

"How do you know all about me? You have been keeping watch on me!" cried Raskolnikov. "I want to know right now—do you suspect me or not?" Raskolnikov brought his fist down on the table. "Arrest me! Search me! But don't play with me! Do you mean to arrest me?"

Just then a noise could be heard through the door. And at that moment a strange thing happened. Neither Raskolnikov nor Porfiry could have imagined such an ending to their meeting.

When he thought about the scene later, this is how Raskolnikov remembered it.

The noise behind the door got louder. Then the door opened a little bit.

"What is it?" cried Porfiry.

Suddenly a very pale man pushed into the room. There was a strange gleam in his eyes. His white lips moved silently. He was dressed like a workman. He was, in fact, the painter, Nikolay, who had been working in the flat in the pawnbroker's building! The painter was very young and very slim. Another man, a guard, followed him into the room. He grabbed Nikolay by the arm, but Nikolay pulled away.

Nikolay suddenly knelt down. "I am guilty! I am the murderer!" he cried.

For ten seconds there was silence.

"What . . . you . . . whom did you kill?" Porfiry asked at last.

Nikolay was silent again for a moment.

"Alyona Ivanovna and her sister Lizaveta. I . . . killed . . . with an axe. Darkness came over me," he added suddenly.

He was still on his knees. Porfiry stood thinking for some moments. Then he waved the guard out of the room and closed the door. He looked at Raskolnikov. Raskolnikov was standing in the corner staring wildly at Nikolay. Porfiry looked from Raskolnikov to Nikolay and then to Raskolnikov again.

" Alone?" Porfiry said at last.

At first Nikolay did not understand the question.

"Did you kill them by yourself?"

"Yes, alone. The other painter had nothing to do with it."

Suddenly Porfiry looked at Raskolnikov again. "This won't do. I'm afraid you must go. Good-bye."

He took Raskolnikov by the arm and showed him the door.

"I suppose you did not expect this," said Raskolnikov. He was very surprised but had gained new courage.

"You did not expect it, either, my friend. See how your hand is shaking."

"You're shaking, too, Porfiry."

"Yes, I am. I didn't expect it. Now, you must go. Until we meet again!"

"I believe we can say *good-bye!*"

"That is in God's hands," muttered Porfiry with a strange smile. "Actually, there are more questions I have to ask you. So we shall meet again. In fact, if it is God's will, we may see a great deal of each other."

Then Porfiry looked closely at Raskolnikov. "Now, you're going to a birthday party?"

"To a funeral," said Raskolnikov.

"Of course, a funeral! Take care of yourself and get well."

Raskolnikov walked straight home. He was very confused. When he got home, he sat on the sofa for a quarter of an hour. He tried to collect his thoughts. Nikolay's confession was a complete surprise to him. Surely they would soon discover that the man was lying and the confession was false. Till then, at least, he was out of danger.

He had a sudden feeling of joy. He wanted to hurry to Katerina's. He would be too late for the funeral. But he could make it to the funeral dinner. And there he would see Sonia.

12 Luzhin's Revenge

The morning after his meeting with Dounia and her mother, Luzhin awoke feeling bad. His pride had been hurt.

"Can it all really be over?" he thought. Then he thought of Raskolnikov. If it were possible to kill Raskolnikov by wishing it, Luzhin would have made the wish.

His thoughts turned to the day ahead. While in St. Petersburg, he was staying with his friend, Lebeziatnikov. Since the man was a neighbor, Lebeziatnikov had been invited to the funeral dinner at Katerina Ivanovna's. Luzhin had learned that Raskolnikov would be at the dinner, too. This gave him an idea.

"Do you know Sonia Marmeladov?" Luzhin asked his friend.

"I do," Lebeziatnikov answered.

"I want to see her."

"What for?" Lebeziatnikov asked with surprise.

"Oh, I just want to. You may be present at the meeting. Otherwise, there's no knowing what you might imagine."

Lebeziatnikov brought Sonia to his house. She came in very much surprised. She was, as usual, very shy. Luzhin greeted her politely. He asked her to sit down across from him at a table. Sonia looked at Lebeziatnikov, at Luzhin, and at some money that was lying on the table.

"First of all, Sonia, please tell Katerina how sorry I am about your father's death," Luzhin said.

"Yes. I will tell her at once." Sonia rose to leave.

"That's not all," Luzhin said. He smiled at her.

Sonia quickly sat back down. Her eyes rested on the gray-and-rainbow-colored money on the table. Then she looked away quickly.

Luzhin continued. "I happened to talk to Katerina yesterday, poor woman. I felt sorry for her. I would like to help her. I believe this whole poor family now depends on you?"

Sonia did not answer. She looked at his face.

"As I have said," Luzhin went on, "I would like to help. I do not, however, want to give money directly to Katerina. She does not spend it wisely. Just look how much money she is spending on this dinner. She does all this while her children have not a crust of bread for tomorrow. I am going to give you a small sum of money to help out Katerina. Please do not say I gave it to you."

Luzhin held out a 10-ruble note. Sonia took it, and jumped up to leave. She felt very confused.

When Sonia had gone, Lebeziatnikov went to Luzhin. "I saw and heard everything," he said. "That is very kind. In spite of all the bad things that happened to you yesterday, you found it in your heart to be kind to someone else!"

Luzhin seemed excited and rubbed his hands together.

Meanwhile, Katerina Ivanovna was busy with her husband's funeral. It would be hard to explain just why she was putting on such a fancy dinner. Perhaps she wanted to show that no one had a right to "turn up his nose" at Marmeladov. Perhaps it was "poor people's pride" that made her spend the last of her money on this dinner. Perhaps she wanted to "do like other people." Also, Katerina Ivanovna was simply not thinking very clearly. Her illness had clouded her mind.

There was wine. There was vodka and rum. There were three or four dishes, and tea for after dinner. Katerina had invited all the lodgers and neighbors. She was disappointed to find that many of the well-to-do ones had turned the invitation down. Many of those who did attend seemed to have little respect. One person appeared in his dressing gown.

Katerina decided that her landlady must be responsible for all this. She must have talked to the other lodgers. She must have told them how Katerina could not pay her rent.

By the time they sat down at the table, Katerina was very upset. The dinner was off to a bad start.

When Raskolnikov came in, Katerina was happy to see him. Here was, at last, an "educated" guest. She made him sit on her left side. Katerina immediately began telling him how her landlady had plotted to spoil the dinner. "It's all her fault," she said. She nodded toward the landlady. Then she broke into a fit of coughing. When she took her handkerchief away from her mouth, it was spotted with blood.

"There she is, at last," Katerina said when the coughing stopped. "Sonia, where have you been?"

Sonia hurried in and sat down beside Raskolnikov.

The dinner did not go well. Some of the guests talked about Marmeladov's drinking. Katerina and the landlady argued loudly and constantly.

Then Luzhin appeared in the doorway. He stood looking at the party with serious eyes. Katerina Ivanovna rushed to him. She was pleased that such a gentleman had come to her dinner.

Luzhin pushed past her. "I must have a word with your stepdaughter, Sonia."

The room grew silent. It seemed this serious businessman had come on an important matter. Raskolnikov, standing beside Sonia, moved to let him pass. Luzhin did not seem to notice him. A minute later Lebeziatnikov appeared in the doorway. He did not come in but stood listening.

"Excuse me, but this is a matter of some importance," said Luzhin. "Sonia," he said, "right after your visit I found that a 100-ruble note was missing from my table. Do you know anything about what happened to it? If you tell me now, the matter will be dropped."

The room was silent. Sonia stood pale, staring at Luzhin.

"I know nothing about it," Sonia whispered at last.

"You know nothing? Think it over. I would not accuse you if I were not sure. I had been counting my money. There were 500 rubles on the table. This included three notes of 100 rubles each. I, out of kindness, gave you a 10-ruble note. When you left, I counted my money again. To my surprise a 100-ruble note had disappeared! I cannot suspect Mr. Lebeziatnikov. I am left with you. Oh, how ungrateful! I invite you in to give your family a 10-ruble present. You repay me by stealing my money. It is too bad! Well, what do you say?"

"I have taken nothing," Sonia whispered in terror. "You gave me 10 rubles. Here it is. Take it."

Sonia pulled the 10-ruble note out of her pocket.

"And you do not admit taking the 100 rubles?"

"Good God!" cried Sonia.

"We shall have to send for the police," said Luzhin.

"I knew she was a thief," cried the landlady.

Katerina suddenly realized what was happening.

She rushed at Luzhin. "You accuse her of stealing?" Then she rushed to Sonia. "Oh, Sonia!" She flung her thin arms around Sonia. She screamed at Luzhin. "Sonia would never take money. Why, she would give away her last penny to help someone. You idiot! Search her! Since she has not left the room, the money would have to be on her! Sonia, turn out your pockets! Look, monster, the pocket is empty. Here is the other pocket! See?"

And Katerina turned Sonia's pockets inside out. But a piece of paper flew out of the right pocket. It landed at Luzhin's feet. Luzhin bent over and picked up the paper with two fingers. He held it up for everyone to see and opened it. It was a 100-ruble note.

"Thief! Out of my lodging," yelled the landlady. "Police!"

"No! I did not take it! I know nothing about it!" Sonia cried. Katerina held her in her arms as if to protect her from the world.

"Sonia, I don't believe it," Katerina cried. "You see I don't believe it. Raskolnikov, why don't you stand up for her?"

Luzhin stole a look at Raskolnikov. Their eyes met. The fire in Raskolnikov's eyes seemed ready to turn him to ashes.

"What evil!" a loud voice cried suddenly in the doorway.

Luzhin looked around quickly.

"What evil!" Lebeziatnikov repeated, staring him straight in the face. Lebeziatnikov strode into the room.

"What do you mean?" asked Luzhin.

"I mean that you are a liar!" said Lebeziatnikov.

"Why, what are you talking about?" asked Luzhin.

Lebeziatnikov turned to the room full of people. "Would you believe it? He himself, with his own hands, gave Sonia that 100-ruble note. I saw it. I'll swear. He did it!"

"Are you crazy?" shouted Luzhin. "She herself said I only gave her a 10-ruble note. How could I have given it to her?"

"I saw it," Lebeziatnikov repeated. "I saw how you slipped it into her pocket. Like a fool, I thought you did it out of kindness. When you were saying goodbye, you held her hand with one hand. With the other, the left, you slipped the note into her pocket. I saw it, and I will swear to it."

Luzhin turned pale.

"What for?" Lebeziatnikov went on. "I don't understand. What made you do such a terrible thing?"

Murmurs of anger were heard from all sides.

"I can explain why he did it," Raskolnikov spoke up in a firm voice. "This gentleman Luzhin was to marry my sister. He quarreled with me and then with my mother and my sister. He knew of my friendship with Sonia. He told my mother and sister that Sonia was a terrible woman. By showing that she was a thief, he could prove himself right and me wrong. He saw that Sonia's happiness was important to me. By hurting her, he could, he believed, hurt me. That was what he was working for. That is the whole reason for this."

Luzhin turned very pale. The people in the room were grumbling and frowning at him. They began shouting threats. One guest picked up a glass and threw it at Luzhin. The glass missed him and hit Katerina's landlady.

Sonia was not able to stand any more. She rushed out of the room and ran home.

The landlady screamed at Katerina, "Out of my lodgings! At once!"

"What? On the day of my husband's funeral the woman throws me and my children into the street? Where am I to go?"

Katerina threw an old green shawl over her head. She made her way through the drunken crowd of lodgers. Crying and sobbing, she ran out into the street.

The landlady continued screaming. The dinner guests argued loudly. "Now it is time for me to go," thought Raskolnikov. And he set off for Sonia's lodgings.

13 The Confession

Now Raskolnikov turned his mind back to his own problems. He *had* to tell Sonia who killed Lizaveta. He had been very excited about the victory over Luzhin. Now, once again, he felt fear. He did not know why he had to tell Sonia the truth. He only knew he must.

When he opened Sonia's door, she looked up at him.

"What would have become of me if not for you?" she asked.

"What if you had gone to prison?" Raskolnikov asked her. "Who would have taken care of Katerina and the children? The landlady has thrown them out!"

"My God!" Sonia cried.

"What if you had known Luzhin's plans, Sonia? What if you had known he might hurt Katerina and the children? What if you had to decide if he should live or die? What if you had to choose between his death or Katerina's? How would you decide which of them was to die?"

Sonia looked at him. "Why do you ask about what could not happen? Who has made me a judge to decide who should live or die? Such things are in God's hands. You are leading up to something. Say what you mean!" She began crying.

"Of course you are right, Sonia." Raskolnikov said. He turned pale. He sat down beside Sonia on the bed. He had felt like this at the moment he stood over the old woman with the axe. He felt that he "must not lose another minute."

"Remember, Sonia, I said that when I came today I would tell you who killed Lizaveta? Well, I have come to tell you."

"How do you know?" she asked. Her face grew paler.

"Guess," he said with a strange smile.

"Why do you frighten me like this?"she asked like a child.

"I must be a great friend of *his*, since I know," Raskolnikov said, staring into her face. "He did not mean to kill Lizaveta. He killed her accidentally. He meant to kill the old woman when she was alone. And then Lizaveta came in—he killed her, too."

Another minute passed. They stared at each other.

"You can't guess, then?" he asked. He felt as if he were throwing himself off a high building.

"N-no," whispered Sonia. She was shaking.

"Take a good look."

As soon as he said this, his heart froze. He looked at her and seemed to see the face of Lizaveta.

Lizaveta had stepped back and held up her hand. This is what Sonia did now. She had the same look of helpless terror.

"Have you guessed?" he whispered at last.

"Good God!" she cried. She sobbed and hid her face in the pillows. Then, suddenly, she fell on her knees in front of him. She took his hands. "What have you done to yourself? There is no one in the world now as unhappy as you!"

A strange, new feeling filled his heart. Two tears came into his eyes.

"You won't leave me, Sonia?" he asked.

"No, no. I will follow you everywhere. Oh, how unhappy I am! What's to be done now? I'll follow you to Siberia!"

At the mention of Siberia and at the thought of prison, Raskolnikov's manner changed. His voice hardened. "Perhaps I don't want to go to Siberia yet, Sonia," he said.

In his changed tone, she seemed to hear the murderer speaking. "He is a murderer," she thought. "Could it be true?"

"How could you?" she said. Then she cried, "You were hungry! It was to help your mother? Yes?"

"No, Sonia," he said. He turned away. "I was not so hungry. I certainly did not want to help my mother. I did not even keep the things I stole. I buried them."

"Then why?"

"Perhaps I wanted to prove myself a great man. Perhaps I wanted to show that I could get rid of anything that stood in my way. Perhaps that is how it was. No, that is all nonsense!"

Sonia looked confused. He looked at her sadly.

"Yes, that is nonsense. You know, of course, that my mother has nothing. I did not want to be a burden on her. I wanted to stay at the university without using all her money. The old woman's money would have paid for my first years at school. Well, that is it . . . that is all."

He struggled for words. Then he let his head sink.

"Oh, that's not it. That's not it," Sonia cried.

"I've only killed a louse, Sonia. She was a useless, harmful creature."

"She was a human being!"

"I know, I know. I am talking nonsense. My head hurts. Maybe I am simply crazy. Perhaps my madness drove me to murder. No, that's not it! Again I am saying it wrong.

"Perhaps I was after power. Power, you know, Sonia, is only for those who have the daring to take it. I wanted to have the *daring*—and I killed her. That was the whole cause of it!"

"Oh, hush!" cried Sonia. "You have turned away from God! You have turned to the devil!"

"I know myself it was the devil leading me. It wasn't to help my mother that I did the murder. That is nonsense. I didn't murder to gain money or power. I did it for myself alone. I wanted to find out whether I was a louse like everybody else or a man. I wanted to find out whether I am a trembling creature or whether I have the *right* . . . "

"To kill? Have the right to kill?" cried Sonia.

"The devil led me because I am a louse, just like all the rest. Did I murder that old woman? I murdered myself, not her! I crushed myself once and for all. What am I to do now, Sonia?"

Sonia jumped up. Her eyes began to shine. "Go this very minute. Stand at the crossroads. Bow down. First kiss the earth. Then say to all men aloud, 'I am a murderer!' Then God will send you life again. Will you go? Will you go?"

"You mean Siberia, Sonia? I must give myself up?" he asked gloomily.

"Suffer for your sin and you will be forgiven!"

"No! I am not going to the police, Sonia. They will laugh. They will call me a fool for murdering her and then hiding all the money under a stone."

"But how will you go on living?" Sonia asked.

"Perhaps I have been unfair to myself. Perhaps I am a man and not a louse. I'll make another fight for it!"

"What a burden to bear, your whole life!"

"I will get used to it. Listen now, Sonia. It is time to talk about facts. The police are after me. I shall not give myself up. I shall make a fight for it. They have no real proof against me. I must be careful though. Sonia, will you come and see me in prison?"

"Oh, I will. I will."

They sat side by side. Raskolnikov felt how much Sonia loved him. Strange to say, he felt her love was a painful burden.

"Sonia, you had better not come see me when I am in prison," he said.

"Here, take this wooden cross," said Sonia. "I have another, a copper one that belonged to Lizaveta. I will wear Lizaveta's now and give you this one."

"Not now, Sonia," said Raskolnikov. "Maybe later."

"Yes, later," said Sonia. "When you go to meet your suffering. Then put it on. We will pray together."

At that moment someone knocked on the door. Sonia rushed to the door in fright. It was Lebeziatnikov. He looked upset.

"Sonia! Katerina Ivanovna has gone out of her mind!"

Sonia screamed.

"We don't know what to do," Lebeziatnikov went on. "She screams that she will take the children and go on the streets. She says they will sing and dance, and she will collect money. She is beating the children, and they are crying."

Sonia grabbed her cloak and ran out of the room. Raskolnikov could not catch up with her. He lost her on the streets. He wandered alone. He wondered why he had gone to her. Why had he confessed? Never had he felt so alone. He heard a voice calling him. It was Lebeziatnikov again.

"I have found them," Lebeziatnikov said. "Sonia has found them, too. Katerina and the children are in the streets. She is rapping on a pan and making the children dance. Come!"

Soon they saw a crowd. Raskolnikov could hear Katerina's hoarse voice and her coughing. Katerina, wearing her green shawl and a crushed straw hat, was rushing at her children. She shouted at them to dance, to sing. She had dressed the children in bright-colored rags. They were crying. Sonia was begging Katerina to stop, to come home with her.

Suddenly the frightened children ran off together down the street. Poor Katerina ran after them, weeping and panting for breath. Sonia rushed after her.

"Come back, children! Come back!" cried Katerina. She stumbled as she ran and fell down.

"She has cut herself! She is bleeding!" cried Sonia.

"She is dying!" someone shouted.

They looked closely at Katerina. She had not been cut. The blood that stained the street red was from her chest.

"Take her to my room!" cried Sonia. "Send for a doctor!"

They carried Katerina to Sonia's lodging. There a crowd gathered outside the door. Among this crowd, Svidrigailov suddenly appeared. Raskolnikov looked at him in surprise.

Katerina had been placed on the sofa. She sat up a little and looked at Sonia. "Where are the children? Oh, here they are. We have been your ruin, Sonia. Well, take them, Sonia. I hand them over to you. Let me die in peace." Her pale, yellow face dropped back. Her mouth fell open. She gave a deep sigh and died.

Sonia fell upon her, sobbing. The children cried loudly.

"Raskolnikov, I must have a word with you." Svidrigailov had come up behind Raskolnikov. "I will pay for a funeral," he said. "I have plenty of money to spare. I will pay to put the children in a good orphanage. I will give 1,500 rubles to each child. Sonia will not have to worry about them. I will help her, too, for she is a good girl, isn't she? Tell your sister how I am spending the money."

"Why are you doing this?" asked Raskolnikov.

"You doubt me!" laughed Svidrigailov. "Can't you believe that I am acting out of kindness? She wasn't a 'louse,' you know." He pointed at the dead woman. "She wasn't a 'louse' like some old pawnbroker."

He said this slyly, keeping his eyes fixed on Raskolnikov. Raskolnikov turned white. Svidrigailov was using *his* words, the words he had spoken to Sonia!

Raskolnikov stepped back and looked wildly at Svidrigailov. "How do you know?" he whispered.

"Why, I lodge on the other side of that wall," said Svidrigailov. "I am a neighbor. Raskolnikov, I told you we should become friends. Well, here we have it. And you will see what an agreeable person I can be. You'll see that you can get along with me!"

14 The Accusation

A strange time began for Raskolnikov. It was as though a fog had fallen upon him. There was no escape. He knew he must make some sort of agreement with Svidrigailov. But when they met, they did not speak of the murder.

Svidrigailov had arranged for Katerina's funeral. He had helped find homes for the children.

Raskolnikov had not spoken to Sonia for days. After the funeral service, he went up to her. She took both his hands and let her head sink on his shoulder. This surprised Raskolnikov. It seemed strange that she did not hate him.

One afternoon the door to Raskolnikov's room opened and Razumihin came in. He seemed upset, but did he not raise his voice. "I am not here to learn your secrets. I have only come to find out once and for all if you are crazy. Only a monster or a madman could treat your mother and sister as you have."

"When did you see them last?" asked Raskolnikov.

"Just now. Your mother has been very ill since yesterday. I went to Sonia's to look for you. You were not there. I saw her crying beside a coffin. Now

I find you here, calmly eating some boiled beef. You are not mad! I would swear you are not. If I could only find out your secret, what is wrong. It must be some nonsense. You are a fine fellow."

"Leave it to time, Razumihin. You'll know it all in time."

"Then there is Dounia," Razumihin said. "Something is wrong. She received a letter today."

"She got a letter?" asked Raskolnikov.

"Yes. It upset her very much. When I spoke of you, she begged me not to. Then she went to her room and locked herself in. Well, I must go back to her now."

He hurried out. Then he suddenly opened the door again.

"Oh, by the way, do you remember that murder? You know, the one Porfiry was looking into, that old woman? Do you know the murderer has been found? He confessed. It was one of those workmen, the painter. What I fool I was. I thought the painters were innocent."

"Who told you?" asked Raskolnikov. "Where did you hear about it?"

"Why, from Porfiry," said Razumihin. "Good-bye now. I'll tell you all about it another time. I'll come again soon."

Raskolnikov was left alone with his thoughts. "How could Porfiry believe that Nikolay, the painter, was guilty? How could he, after their meeting and the words that had passed between them? A long time had passed since that meeting—too long a time. There had been not a word from Porfiry. Well, that was a bad sign."

Raskolnikov took his cap and went out of the room. "I must settle things with Svidrigailov," he thought. "He, too, seems to be waiting for me to come to him." At that moment he felt a rush of hate for the two men—Svidrigailov and Porfiry. He felt he could kill either one.

Raskolnikov had just left his room when he stumbled upon Porfiry in the hall. The police investigator was coming to see him. Raskolnikov was not very much surprised at seeing Porfiry. "Perhaps this will mean the end," he thought.

"You did not expect a visitor?" Porfiry said, laughing. I have been meaning to stop in. I was just passing by. I won't keep you long."

"Come in, Porfiry. Sit down." Raskolnikov put on a pleased and friendly look.

Porfiry sat down and began lighting a cigarette.

"Speak, speak!" seemed as though it would burst from Raskolnikov's heart. "Come, why don't you speak?"

"My doctor tells me I should give up smoking," said Porfiry. "I know it is bad for me, yet I can't give it up."

"He is playing his tricks again," thought Raskolnikov.

"I have come to have it out with you, Raskolnikov," Porfiry said suddenly. "I owe you an explanation."

A serious look came over the man's face. To his surprise, Raskolnikov saw a touch of sadness in it.

"I liked you from the moment I met you, Raskolnikov," he said. "I saw a touch of greatness in you. Who knows what might have come of our meeting if Nikolay had not burst in?"

"Razumihin told me that you think Nikolay is guilty," said Raskolnikov.

"I had to put Razumihin off," said Porfiry. "But never mind him. Let's speak of Nikolay. Did you know Nikolay belongs to the religious group called the Wanderers? These people believe that they must 'suffer.' If they suffer at the hands of authority, so much the better. I suspect that Nikolay now simply wants to 'suffer.' He wants to be put into prison, to be punished, so that he can suffer. I know it for certain. Only he doesn't know that I know. When I question him on some facts of the murder, he simply does not know the facts!"

Raskolnikov shook as if he had been stabbed. "Then—who is the murderer?" he asked in a breathless voice.

Porfiry sank back in his chair as though he were amazed at the question.

"Who is the murderer?" he repeated, as though unable to believe his ears. "Why, *you* , Raskolnikov! You are the murderer," he added in a whisper.

Raskolnikov jumped from the sofa. He stood for a few seconds, and then he sat back down without a word. His face twitched.

"Your lip is twitching just as it did at our last meeting," said Porfiry, almost kindly. "I came to tell you everything and deal with you openly."

"I did not murder her," whispered Raskolnikov. He was like a frightened child caught in the act.

"No, it was you, Raskolnikov. You and no one else," Porfiry whispered sternly.

They were both silent. The silence lasted a long time, almost ten minutes.

"I don't want you to look on me as a monster," Porfiry said at last. "I've come to you because I have a real liking for you. I've come to tell you that you should confess. It will be better for you. I promise you that."

Raskolnikov thought for a long time. At last he smiled, and his smile was sad and gentle.

"No!" he said. "It is not worth it! I don't care about getting a shorter jail sentence. When do you mean to arrest me?"

"Well, I can let you walk about another day or two. Think it over, my dear fellow."

"And what if I run away?" asked Raskolnikov with a strange smile.

"You won't run away," said Porfiry. "I believe you will decide to take your suffering. You don't believe my words now. But you will. For suffering, Raskolnikov, is a great thing."

Raskolnikov got up and picked up his cap.

"Are you going for a walk? The evening will be fine if we don't have a storm. Though a storm would be a good thing to freshen the air."

Porfiry, too, took his cap.

"Porfiry, please don't imagine that I have confessed to you today. You are a strange man, and I have listened to you out of simple curiosity. But I have admitted nothing."

"Oh, I know that. Look at you. You are trembling. So, I will go. Until we meet again! May you have good thoughts and make the right decisions."

Porfiry went out without looking at Raskolnikov again. Raskolnikov went to the window and watched. He waited until Porfiry had reached the street and walked away. Then he too went quickly out of the room.

15 Svidrigailov Meets His End

Raskolnikov hurried to Svidrigailov's. On the way, one question worried him: had Svidrigailov been to see Porfiry? As far as Rakolnikov could tell, he had not. But would Svidrigailov go to Porfiry? Oh, how sick he was of the whole thing!

A thought played in Raskolnikov's mind. Svidrigailov was a very unpleasant person. Terrible stories were told about his past. Svidrigailov had found out his secret. What if he were to use the secret as a weapon against Dounia? The thought filled Raskolnikov with rage. Would he have to give himself up to save Dounia?

What about the letter? This morning Dounia had received a letter. Who would send her a letter?

He must see Svidrigailov as soon as possible. If he really were plotting against Dounia, then— Raskolnikov could only come up with one answer. "Then I shall kill him."

As he walked down the street, Raskolnikov saw Svidrigailov. He was sitting at a table by the window of a tavern. When Svidrigailov saw that Raskolnikov had spotted him, he broke into a sly grin. "Well, well, come in if you want me. I am here!" he shouted.

Raskolnikov went into the tavern. He sat down with Svidrigailov and stared at his face. It was like a mask—white and red, with bright red lips, and a pale beard and hair. His eyes were somehow too blue. There was something awful in that handsome face, which looked so wonderfully young for his age.

"So I have to worry about you now, too," Raskolnikov said. "Don't think what you know about me will help you get to my sister. Don't try anything of the sort. I will kill you before they can lock me up."

When Svidrigailov spoke, he changed the subject. "How do you feel about women, Raskolnikov? Women are my weakness in this world. It was for women that I came to St. Petersburg. Do you know how attracted I was to your sister? The very rustle of her dress as she passed was more than I could stand. If she had told me to poison my wife so we could be together, I would have done it at once! But you know how badly that all ended."

Raskolnikov saw that wine was beginning to affect Svidrigailov. He was talking freely.

"Well, after what you have said, I'm sure you have come to St. Petersburg with plans for my sister," Raskolnikov said.

"Nonsense," said Svidrigailov. "Your sister can't stand me. Besides, don't you remember I told you that I am to be married? It has all been arranged.

117

The girl will be 16 in another month. She is simply beautiful! I gave her a gift of diamonds and pearls. She flung her little arms around me and promised she would be a good, obedient wife. It's worth paying for, isn't it?"

"Will you really marry such a young girl?"

"Why, of course. I am a sinful man. Ha-ha-ha! But enough. I must go. Sorry I can't talk longer, but I will see you again."

Svidrigailov walked out of the tavern. Raskolnikov followed him.

"I am not going to lose sight of you," cried Raskolnikov. "From your drunken stories, I am sure you have plans for my sister! She received a letter this morning. You may intend to marry, but that means nothing."

"I am going to get a carriage and go see my young bride. You can come with me if you like," said Svidrigailov.

Svidrigailov hailed a carriage and climbed inside. Raskolnikov decided that, for the time at least, Svidrigailov would be busy. He turned and walked away. If he had only turned around, he might have seen Svidrigailov get out of the carriage and send it on its way.

As Raskolnikov walked across a nearby bridge, he passed his sister Dounia. He walked right by without seeing her. Dounia was surprised. She did not know whether to call his name or not. Just then she saw Svidrigailov. He was standing on the sidewalk before the bridge. He was signaling to her. Dounia went to him.

"Let us hurry away," Svidrigailov whispered to her. "I don't want Raskolnikov to know of our meeting. He has somehow heard of my letter to you and suspects me of something. You didn't tell him about it, did you?"

"No. We have turned the corner. My brother can't see us now. Tell me what you have to say here in the street. I will go no farther with you," Dounia said.

"In the first place, I cannot tell you here in the street. In the second place, you must hear Sonia, too. If you won't come with me, I will tell you nothing. But don't forget, this is a very important secret that your beloved brother is keeping."

Dounia stared at Svidrigailov.

"What are you afraid of?" he asked. "We won't be alone. Sonia is home next door. Am I really so terrible?"

Svidrigailov's lips twisted in a smile.

"I know that you are not a man of honor. However, I am not afraid of you. Lead the way," she said calmly. But her face was pale.

Svidrigailov stopped at Sonia's room first. "Oh, she is not at home. Well, she may return soon. Here is my flat." He unlocked the door and showed Dounia in. "Notice it is directly next to Sonia's room. Her room is on the other side of this wall. See how a chair stands next to that locked door? I sat on that chair listening to Sonia talk to your brother. I sat there listening on two evenings. And I was able to learn something. Now, come sit down."

Svidrigailov sat at least seven feet away from Dounia. But there was a glow in his eye that made her shudder.

"Here is your letter," she said. "You hint at a crime committed by my brother. I don't believe you."

"I have his own words as proof. He came here on two evenings to see Sonia. He confessed to her. He is a murderer. He killed an old woman, a pawnbroker, with an axe. He killed her sister, too, a peddler named Lizaveta. He murdered them to rob them. He told all this to Sonia. She is the only person who knows his secret. She was as horrified as you are now. But don't worry. She won't tell."

"It cannot be," said Dounia. "It's a lie! Why would he do such a thing?"

"He explained it all to Sonia. Something about a theory that great men have the right to get rid of things in their way. He had some kind of idea about dividing people into groups. He said something about superior people not having to obey the law. You are very pale, Dounia."

"I know his theory," she said. "I read that article of his about extraordinary men. Razumihin brought it to me. I want to see Sonia!" She got up to leave.

"I know Sonia will not be back until night."

"Ah, then you were lying! You were lying!" Dounia cried.

"Calm yourself, Dounia. Come, would you like me to help your brother? I could pay for him to go abroad. He may be a great man yet. Where are you going?"

"To my brother. Why is this door locked? We came in that door and now it is locked."

"Sit down. Calm down." Svidrigailov said. "Let us think about how we can save your brother."

"How can you save him? Can he be saved?"

"It all depends on you, on you alone," Svidrigailov whispered. His eyes glowed. "One word from you and he is saved. I have money. I will get him a passport. What do you want with Razumihin? I love you. I love you beyond everything. I love the rustle of your dress. I will kiss the hem. I'll do anything for you."

Dounia rushed to the door again. "Open it! Open it!" she cried, shaking the door. "This is an outrage!"

She rushed to the farthest corner of the room and hid behind a table. She stared at Svidrigailov, watching every move he made.

"Think about it," Svidrigailov said with a smile. "Your brother's fate is in your hands. I will be your slave. No one is home in the building. There is no one to hear you."

Dounia knew her words were useless. She knew Svidrigailov. Suddenly she pulled a small gun out of her pocket.

"So that's it, is it!" Svidrigailov cried. He was surprised but still smiling. "Where did you get the gun?"

"It belonged to your wife, you scoundrel! I took it when I began to suspect that you were after me. If you come one step closer, I will kill you!"

"Well then, shoot, you pretty, wild creature. Shoot!"

Dounia raised the gun. Deathly pale, she stared at him. Fire glowed in her eyes. He had never seen her look so beautiful. He took a step forward, and a shot rang out. A bullet grazed his hair. It flew into the wall. He stood still and laughed softly.

"What's this? Blood?" He took out a handkerchief and wiped a thin trail of blood from his head. The bullet had just scratched his skin. He moved closer. "Well, now you can hardly miss me." His eyes were wild. Dounia saw he would rather die than let her go. Suddenly she flung the gun away.

He went to Dounia and gently put his arm around her waist. She trembled like a leaf.

"Let me go," she begged.

Svidrigailov shuddered. "Then you don't love me?"

Dounia shook her head.

"And you can't . . . never?"

"Never!"

There followed a moment of struggle in Svidrigailov's heart. Suddenly he let her go. He turned quickly to the window and stood facing it. Another moment passed.

"Here is the key." He took it out of his pocket and laid it on the table. "Take it! Make haste!"

Dounia grabbed the key. She flew to the door, unlocked it, and rushed out of the room.

Svidrigailov stayed at the window for a few minutes. Then he turned. A strange smile was on his face. The gun lay on the floor. He picked it up and looked at it. There were still two bullets left in it. He put the gun in his pocket, took his hat, and left.

He spent that rainy evening going from one tavern to another. Then he went home and gathered together all his money. He went to Sonia's room. She had returned.

Svidrigailov sat down at her table. "I may be going to America, Sonia," he said. "Here are 3,000 rubles. You will need the money now. You must not go on earning a living in the old way."

"I can't take this," Sonia said.

"You will need it. Raskolnikov has two choices: a bullet in the brain or Siberia."

Sonia looked wildly at him.

"I know all about it. Raskolnikov himself has told me. I won't tell anyone. You gave him good advice when you told him to confess. If he goes to Siberia, you will need money to follow him. You'll need it for him. My giving it to you is the same as giving it to him. Don't say anything about this. Well, I will be on my way."

He went out, leaving Sonia very upset.

Svidrigailov made one more visit that evening. He went through the rain to see the girl he was to marry. He told her he must leave St. Petersburg. He gave her a present of 15,000 rubles. He patted her cheek and said he would return.

Then Svidrigailov went back to his rooms and fell asleep. He had nightmares. He dreamed of a young, beautiful girl lying dead in her coffin. Svidrigailov knew the girl. She had drowned herself. She was only 14, but her heart had been broken. Her innocence had been stolen on a wet, cold, dark night.

When Svidrigailov woke, he put on his wet overcoat. He took a notebook out of his pocket and wrote a few lines on the first page. He read them over. Then he walked out of the room.

The street was deserted. It was cold and wet. At last he came to a big stone house. There a little man stood wearing a very big overcoat. He looked at Svidrigailov, who came up close to him.

"What do you want?" the man asked.

"I am going to foreign parts," answered Svidrigailov.

"To foreign parts?"

"To America."

Svidrigailov took out the gun.

The man looked shocked. "I say, this is not the place for such jokes!" he cried.

"Well, brother, it is a good place. When you are asked, just say he said he was going to America."

Svidrigailov put the gun to his own right temple.

"You can't do that here!" cried the man.

Svidrigailov pulled the trigger.

16 The Truth Comes Out

That same day Raskolnikov was on his way to his mother's and sister's lodgings. It was evening, and he found his mother at home alone.

Raskolnikov's clothes were torn and dirty. They were soaked with the night's rain. He had spent the night before wandering. And he had reached a decision.

Pulcheria was so happy to see him. She took him by the hands and drew him into the room.

"Here you are!" she began. "I am laughing, not crying. I am so delighted. Oh, how muddy you are! Were you in the rain?

"But I do not plan to question you, my boy," she went on. "I am just glad you are here. I was reading the article you wrote."

Raskolnikov took the magazine his mother held. He glanced at his article.

"My goodness! Why am I sitting here?" Pulcheria said. "There is coffee. I'll get it at once."

"Mother, don't trouble. I am going. Listen, mother. Whatever happens, whatever you hear about me, will you always love me as you do now?" he asked.

"How can you ask me such a question? Who will tell me anything about you? Besides, I wouldn't believe anyone!"

"I've come to tell you that I have always loved you. And that you must always believe your son loves you."

Pulcheria hugged him tightly. "I don't know what is wrong with you, son," she said at last. "Last night Dounia talked of you in her sleep. I felt all morning as if I were waiting for something terrible to happen. But where are you going? You are going away somewhere?"

"Yes."

"I can come with you. Dounia would come, too. We could bring Sonia along if you wish."

"Good-bye, mother. Kneel down and pray to God for me."

"Let me bless you and sign you with the cross," she said.

Raskolnikov was very glad that he was alone with his mother. For the first time in all those awful months, his heart softened. He fell down before her. He kissed her feet. They both cried.

"I won't question you," his mother said. "Only tell me, are you going very far?"

"Very far."

"Not forever? You will come one more time, tomorrow?"

"I will, I will, good-bye." Raskolnikov tore himself away.

It was a fresh, bright evening. It had cleared up that morning. When Raskolnikov returned to his own room, he found Dounia there. She was sitting alone, deep in thought. When she looked up, her eyes were filled with horror. He saw at once that she knew.

"I have been with Sonia," she said. "Where have you been?"

"I don't remember clearly. I wanted to make up my mind once and for all. I walked by the river. I remember I wanted to end it all there. But—I couldn't make up my mind."

"Thank God! That is just what Sonia and I were afraid of. Then you still have faith in life? Thank God!"

"I have just been weeping in my mother's arms."

"Have you been at mother's? Have you told her?" cried Dounia in horror.

"No, I didn't tell her. But she understood a great deal. I am a terrible person, Dounia."

"Terrible, but ready to face suffering! You are, aren't you?"

"Yes, I am going. I am going to give myself up. But I don't know why I am going to give myself up."

Big tears fell down Dounia's cheeks.

"You are crying, sister. Can you hold your hands out to me?"

"You doubted it?" She threw her arms around him.

"Dounia, go. Sit with mother. She needs you. Razumihin will be there, too. Don't cry about me."

At last they both went out. Dounia walked away but turned to look back at him. He looked at her, too. For the last time, their eyes met. Then he waved her away and quickly turned the corner.

What would 15 or 20 years of prison do to him, he wondered. Wouldn't it crush him completely? Then why should he go now? It was the hundredth time that he had asked himself that question that day. But still, he went.

He went to Sonia's room. It was getting dark. Sonia had been waiting for him all day. When he walked in, Sonia gave a cry of joy. But when she looked carefully at his face, she turned pale.

"Yes," said Raskolnikov. "I have come for your cross, Sonia. It was you who told me to go to the crossroads. Why are you frightened now that the time has come?"

Sonia looked at him. His tone seemed strange.

"I am not going to Porfiry. I am sick of him. I will go to some other policeman."

Raskolnikov talked rapidly, and his hands were shaking.

Without a word, Sonia took two crosses out of the drawer. One was made of wood and one was made of copper. She put the wooden cross on his neck.

"So, it is the symbol of my taking up the cross," he said. "Why are you crying? You are looking at me like my mother or Dounia."

"Cross yourself. At least say one prayer," Sonia begged.

He crossed himself. Sonia picked up a green shawl and put it over her head. Raskolnikov realized that she planned to go with him.

"Where are you going? Stay here! I will go alone!"

He went out. Sonia stood in the middle of the room. He had not even said good-bye to her.

As Raskolnikov walked, he remembered Sonia's words: "Stand at the crossroads. Bow down. First kiss the earth. Then say to all men aloud, 'I am a murderer!'" He trembled remembering that. Tears came to his eyes. He fell to the earth. He knelt down and kissed the filthy earth.

"He's drunk!" a young boy near him said. There was a roar of laughter.

The remarks and laughter stopped Raskolnikov. The words 'I am a murderer'" died away before he spoke them. Without looking around, he turned down the street that led to the police office.

He had seen something that did not surprise him. When he knelt down, he caught sight of Sonia. She was hidden a short distance from him, watching. She had followed him. Raskolnikov knew then, once and for all, that Sonia was with him forever. She would

131

follow him to the ends of the earth. She would follow him wherever fate might take him.

He reached the police office. He had to climb three flights up. His legs were weak. He stopped for a moment to catch his breath, to enter *like a man*. He entered the office.

"Yes, what is it?" an officer asked. "Are you here on business? What is your name?"

"Raskolnikov."

"Yes, Raskolnikov. You have been here before. I remember you. I have heard of you. Ah, we have had a busy day. A suicide, only this morning. Some gentleman who had just come to town shot himself. What was his name?" The officer turned to another policeman.

"Svidrigailov," someone answered from another desk.

Raskolnikov was startled. "Svidrigailov! Svidrigailov has shot himself!" he cried.

"What? Do you know Svidrigailov?"

"Yes, I knew him. He hasn't been here long."

"Right. He lost his wife not long ago. He was a man of wild habits. All of a sudden he shot himself. He left in his notebook a few words. He wrote that he died knowing what he was doing and that no one is to blame for his death. You know him? Then you can tell us something about him?"

"I saw him yesterday. He was drinking wine. I know nothing."

Raskolnikov felt as though something were choking him.

"You've turned pale," the officer said. "It's so stuffy in here."

"Yes, I must go," whispered Raskolnikov.

He went out. He had to hold on to the wall as he went down the stairs. He went into the yard. There, not far from the entrance, stood Sonia. She was pale. She looked wildly at him. He looked at her, and then he went back into the police office.

"Hello? Back again?" said the officer. "What is the matter?"

Raskolnikov stared with wide eyes and white lips. He walked closer to the table, and leaned on it. He tried to say something, but could not.

"You are feeling ill. Have a chair."

"It was I . . . " began Raskolnikov.

"Drink some water."

Raskolnikov waved the water away. Softly and brokenly, but very clearly, he said . . .

"It was I who killed the old pawnbroker woman and her sister Lizaveta. I killed them with an axe and robbed them."

The police officer opened his mouth. People ran up on all sides.

Raskolnikov repeated his statement.

Epilogue

Siberia. On the banks of a lonely river stands a town. In the town there is a prison. In the prison convict Raskolnikov has been for nine months. Almost a year and a half has passed since his crime.

There had been little difficulty with his trial. He had confessed everything. He had clearly given all the details. The judges noted that he had not kept any of the stolen things. He had never opened the purse and did not even know how much money he had taken. They decided he must have been out of his mind and that he was very sorry for his crime. Witnesses told of noble things Raskolnikov had done in his life. Indeed, he once saved two children from a burning building. Raskolnikov's sentence was a light one.

At the very beginning of the trial, Raskolnikov's mother fell ill. Her illness was a strange one. She seemed rather out of her mind. Dounia and Razumihin had made up a story to protect her from the truth about Raskolnikov. They told her he was off on secret business. Strangely, Pulcheria asked few questions about her son. She said only that she knew that someday he would be a great man. She spent her days reading and rereading his article.

With the money left to her by Svidrigailov, Sonia prepared to follow Raskolnikov to Siberia.

Two months after the trial, Dounia and Razumihin were married. It was a quiet, sad wedding. Pulcheria gave them her blessing.

A short time later, Pulcheria died. In a fever before her death, she said some strange words. They showed she knew more about her son's terrible fate than people had supposed.

Sonia had settled into the town and taken a job as a dressmaker. She wrote to Dounia and Razumihin from Siberia. She sent news of Raskolnikov. He was a quiet, sullen prisoner. He was not friendly with any of the other prisoners. He was, in fact, quite rude and unkind to her. Still she visited him as often as she was allowed.

In one letter, Sonia wrote that Raskolnikov had fallen ill and was in the prison hospital. While he was in the hospital, Sonia continued her visits. Then one day she did not come. She did not come the next day, nor the next. Raskolnikov felt uneasy. Something seemed to stab him in the heart.

He was discharged from the hospital and sent back to the prison. There he learned that Sonia was ill. After asking questions, he learned that her illness was not serious. At last Sonia sent him a note. She had a cold, she wrote, and would be back to see him soon.

It was a bright, warm day. Early in the morning, Raskolnikov went to work on the riverbank with two other prisoners. Suddenly he found Sonia beside him. She wore her green shawl, and her thin face showed signs of illness. She smiled and held out her hand as usual. Often, Raskolnikov had refused to take her hand. He seemed angry at her visits. But now he took her hand and did not let go. He looked at her, and then he dropped his eyes to the ground without speaking. They were alone. The guard had turned away for the time being.

All at once something seemed to seize him and fling him at her feet. He cried and threw his arms around her. A light of joy came into her eyes. She knew that he loved her beyond everything.

Tears filled their eyes. They were both pale and thin, but their faces were bright with love.

They would wait. They would be patient. They had another seven years to wait—but what happiness was before them! Seven years, *only* seven years!

Raskolnikov did not know that this new life would not come easily. He would have to work hard and suffer greatly. But that is the beginning of a new story—the story of a new, unknown life for Raskolnikov. Our present story has ended.